施璐德亚洲有限公司 编
岑品杰 译

施璐德年鉴 2022

VISION
DRIVEN
LIFE

CNOOD 2008 TO 2022

復旦大學出版社

CNOOD Yearbook
(2022)

目录

1

人生三修
The Three-Fold Self-Cultivation of Life
Zhengyu Ding

21

迎潮而上，顺势而为
Ride the Tide, and Seize the Momentum
Lin Zhang

62

接纳普通，有度的人生更自在
Accepting Ordinariness, a Moderate Life Is More Comfortable
Andy Wei

73

CNOOD 十年，我的十年
My Ten Years at CNOOD
Belinda Chen

88

新岁序开，同赴新程
A New Year Begins with A New Journey Ahead
CNOOD News

104

记施璐德"予她闪耀"秋日主题活动
The CNOOD Fall Themed Event of "Let Her Shine"
CNOOD News

116

梦一样的 2022 年
2022: A Year Like a Dream
Tommy Chen

119

立春到，万物兴
As Spring Sets In, Everything Prospers
Jerry Dai

122
春暖花会开
We Shall See Flowers in Bloom When It's Springtime
Jenna Hu

125
满怀希望方可所向披靡
Be Hopeful, Be Invincible
Hogan He

130
金山城市沙滩
Jinshan City Beach
Cici Kang

132
一直在路上
Always on the Road
David Lee

143
随　想
Random Thoughts
Joanna Lee

147
随　笔
Some Short Notes
Roger Lee

149
让成长一路荣光，为梦想不负芳华
May Our Path of Growth Be Full of Glory, and Seize the Days for Our Dreams
William Qiu

152
2023 年，再次出发
2023, It's Time to Start Over
Johnson Shen

157
十年施璐德
A Decade with CNOOD
Andy Wei

161
德意志列车
The German Trains
Mira Wei

165
迎接 2023 年
Welcome to 2023
Amanda Wu

171
幸福在哪里
Where Is Happiness
Ada Wang

174
2022 年生活中那些阶段性的思考
2022: Some Reflections at Certain Stages of Life
Cassie Chen

177
2023 春节有感
The Spring Festival of 2023
Liam Wu

180
2022 年有感
My Reflections on 2022
Danni Xu

185
笃行逐梦　不负韶华
Be Honest in Your Pursuit of Dreams, and Waste Not the Days of Youth
Heather Zhang

188
回首 2022 年
Looking Back on 2022
Jodie Zhou

191
四十不惑
At the Age of Forty
James Zhu

人生三修
The Three-Fold Self-Cultivation of Life

■ Zhengyu Ding

我过去在世界500强的德国公司工作，2008年施璐德亚洲有限公司创建前，我就结识了创始人池勇海博士，尽管我们之间多年来没达成过任何业务合作，但因志趣相投成为好朋友。记得池总创建公司之初，就向我发出过邀请，希望我加入施璐德一起创业，虽然施璐德开出的条件很好，但我那时还没有跳槽的打算，而且还要照顾家庭。

直到2020年7月8日，退休两个月后，我才正式走进施璐德。后来公司开会时老池偶尔也会开玩笑："丁总，当时邀请你来，你不愿意来，嫌我们庙太小。"

我也开玩笑说："我没来损失可大了，财富值少了一个亿。"

I used to work for a Fortune 500 company from Germany and got to know Dr. Dennis Chi, the founder of CNOOD ASIA LIMITED, before its founding in 2008. Being like-minded, we became good friends though we didn't enter into any business cooperation. I still remember that Dennis invited me to join CNOOD to start a business with him. Though CNOOD offered me very good terms, I did not have a plan of changing my job and had to look after my family at that time.

It was not until July 8, 2020, two months after my retirement, that I joined CNOOD. In later days, Dennis would sometimes say to me jokingly at meetings, "Mr. Ding, when I invited you at that time, you were unwilling to come because our company was too small for you."

I would reply with a joke, "I must have lost a lot because didn't come earlier. I guess there was a one-hundred-million

1. 梅开二度，全新纪年

这两句玩笑话，既映射出我们因缘相识15年的情谊，又反映了施璐德十多年间迅猛发展。施璐德是一家多元化公司，与其说是公司，不如说是一个商业平台。这个平台是开放包容的，你想到的想不到的项目都可能出现在这里。池总搭建这个平台，让大家在平台上各取所需，各展所长。在这里一切靠自律，你要知道自己想干什么事，而不是等着别人告诉你该做什么事。这样的经营理念和模式，在国内为数不多，也是吸引我的原因之一。

loss in my total wealth."

I. A New Start of My Career

The joke reflects not only the 15 years of friendship since we got to know each other, but also the rapid growth of CNOOD in more than a decade. CNOOD is a diversified company. In fact, it is more a business platform than a company. This platform is open and inclusive, with any project you may think of or even beyond your imagination. Dennis has built this platform so that everyone can take what they need and display what they are good at doing. Here, everything depends on self-discipline; you must know what you want to do, rather than wait for others to tell you what to do. Such philosophy and mode of business is quite rare in China, which is one of the reasons why I was

进入施璐德后，我成为采购中心总经理，工作内容及流程相对熟悉，基本不需要适应期。我的核心目标就是"开疆拓土，构建网络"八个字。在创业型公司做事，说使出浑身解数也不为过，要充分调动积极性和主观能动性。为了拓展业务，我开始梳理自己的人脉，将其构建成网络。进施璐德前，我也问过自己，毕竟是退休的人，"廉颇老矣，尚能饭否"？但老有老的价值，同样的位置，我接手后可以直接推进项目，刚毕业的大学生也许只能开展项目，性质和进程就完全不同了。

老池是一个梦想家，他的大脑就像宇宙，总是有各种点子冒出来。有时你还在陆地上，他已经搭火箭去了太空。也正是因为这样，他对人才的渴求度更高，需要各个领域的造梦师来同他一起实现梦想。他对人才的重视从不断向我发出入职邀约就可以看得出来。老池在意"一城一池"，锚定了就会选择各种时机出手，但他又绝不在意"一城一池"的得失，就算被拒绝，"城池"就在这，总有机会能实现目标。这一点也看出老池是一个极为有韧性、有可持续意识的人。

attracted to CNOOD.

I became the general manager of the Purchasing Center after I joined CNOOD. I was relatively familiar with the job and its process, and basically didn't need the time to adapt to the new environment. My core goal could be summarized as "pushing the frontiers and building a network." Working in a start-up company, it is not too much to say that we have to exert ourselves to the utmost and fully mobilize our enthusiasm and initiative. To expand the business, I began to sort out my personal connections and build them into a network. Before I joined CNOOD, I asked myself whether I was still capable of doing a job well as a retired person. However, senior citizens have their own merits. As for a same position, I'm able to advance a project directly after taking it over, while newly graduates may only be able to execute it. So things will be different both in nature and process.

Dennis is a dreamer with a brain like the universe, from which all kinds of ideas are popping up all the time. Sometimes you are still on the ground when he has already gone to the space in a rocket. As a result, he has a keener thirst for talented people and needs dream-makers from all fields to realize dreams with him. The importance he attaches to talented people is evident from the fact that he kept sending me offers to join the company. He pays great attention to every "fortress" and will find every opportunity to make a

基于此，施璐德不断引进人才，不仅从各个领域挖掘人才，也招募管培生，给机会，给权限，大力培养。我们以前经常开玩笑说，施璐德很像过去的黄埔军校，入学时是精英，学成即是将领，无论去到哪个领域都游刃有余。所以在这里，员工的企业忠诚度较高，很多员工在这里工作十年以上。这对于一家创业型公司来讲，实属难得。

2. 商海无涯，真诚为舟

从德国公司到施璐德，几十年职场打拼总结出的经验，就是要建立广博的人脉网络，这件事说复杂很复杂，说简单也可以很简单，于我而言就是恪守两个字：真诚。对人一定要真诚！

有人的世界，沟通很重要，事情做不好、做不成，大部分都和沟通有关。无论面对朋友还是供应商，沟通都是首要

move once he locates a target; however, he never cares about the gain or loss of any single "fortress." Even if he is rejected, the "fortress" is still here, and there is always a chance to achieve the goal. We can see that Dennis is an extremely resilient person with an awareness of sustainability.

Therefore, CNOOD has been constantly bringing in talented people, seeking out professionals from various fields as well as recruiting management trainees. It provides opportunities and gives powers to them, while devoting major efforts to their training. We used to joke that CNOOD was very much like the Whampoa Military Academy in the past, where cadets were elites when they were enrolled and generals when they graduated. They can do their jobs perfectly well whatever field they are in. Therefore, here at CNOOD employees are generally high-loyalty employees, many of whom have been working here for more than ten years. This is indeed rare for a start-up company.

II. The Importance of Being Sincere in the Business World

The experience of my decades-long career, from the German company to CNOOD, boils down to one point: building an extensive network of personal connections. This is very complicated but at the same time quite simple; for me it means always sticking to one principle: sincerity. You must be sincere to all!

的。像我目前所在的部门,主要业务是采购各类项目所需的材料或部件。我们常会遇到这样的情况,昨天刚刚谈好的采购价格今天就涨了,那怎么办?此时如果想法偏颇、做法激烈,那损失的不仅是一个项目,更是未来很多的可能性。

所以,不仅要经营项目,更要经营关系。我们提倡透明和互信。做生意势必会考虑利润,但要在合理的范围内,一锤子买卖和持续合作的性质是不同的,做事方

Communication is important in the human society. In most cases, it is because of the problem of communication that we fail to do something well or achieve expected goals. Whether we are dealing with a friend or a supplier, communication is always of the first importance. The main task of the department I'm now working in is to purchase various types of materials or components for the projects. We often meet such a situation: yesterday we reached an agreement on the procurement price, and yet it goes up today. What should we do then? In this case, if we take drastic actions with biased views, we will lose not only a project but also future possibilities.

Therefore, it is necessary to manage relationships as well as projects. We call for transparency and mutual trust. Of course we must consider our profit when

式自然也不同。如果我们以可持续意识做生意，那我们跟供应商之间、跟客户之间就不只是供给关系，而是类似战略合作伙伴的关系。

我进入施璐德后逐步开发的客户有一部分是之前就认识的，多年一直保持良好的关系，所以换一个新平台来合作，有熟悉的可信任的人，平台能提供的条件也不错，事情就更容易推进。

doing business, but it has to be reasonable. The nature of a one-off deal and an ongoing partnership are different, with different ways of doing things. If we do business with a sense of sustainability, we will be able to build a relationship with our suppliers and with our clients; it is not just a relationship of demand and supply, but one that is similar to a strategic partnership.

Among the clients I have gradually developed since I joined CNOOD, some are my old acquaintances, with whom I have maintained good relationships for many years. It is easier to get things done when we just switch to a new platform with old friends who are trustworthy and good conditions the platform can provide.

就像老池写的那本《共同利益论》所言，天平双方要秉持的核心是"双赢"，单赢很难平衡，时间久了，"付出"和"好"都容易变成忍气吞声，一旦发心变了，关系也就岌岌可危，事情也没办法做好。所以，我们现在同客户进行业务往来，在彼此了解的基础上，利润是最基本的保障，在此基础上建立互信。生意做到最后事情只是一方面，做事的人是另一方面。人对了，即使当下事不对，也总能向对的方向走。

Just as Dennis wrote in his book *Common Interest Theory*, "win-win" is the core principle for both sides; it is difficult to maintain the balance if it is a win-lose situation, in which "sacrifice" and "kindness" would easily become suffering in silence. Once we deviate from the original aspiration, the mutual relationship will be in jeopardy, and there is no way to do things well. Therefore, when doing business with our clients, profit is the basic guarantee, followed by mutual trust. In the end, the work itself is only one side of business, while the person who does the work is the other. Though we might have problems with the work, we can always move toward the right direction if we have the right person doing the job.

3. 铺未来路，做进阶梯

过去在德国公司，工作氛围是严肃和严谨的，不能有一丝懈怠。这样谨小慎微工作二十多年，对身体和精神都是极大考验。来到施璐德后，反而激发了我的潜在活力，更喜欢开疆拓土，喜欢和年轻人一起在冲锋的路上。

每天跟年轻人在一起，各方面体验都很好。施璐德的年轻人不骄不躁，对我很尊重，我对他们也以爱护之心对待，很多同事私下里叫我老顽童。总之，工作氛围很好，简单，基本没什么矛盾。大家共享资源，只一门心思把事做好。当然，这也跟施璐德的企业文化分不开。

III. Paving the Way for the Future and the Young

When I worked in the German company, where the working atmosphere was serious and rigorous, even the slightest slackness was not tolerated. Working meticulously like this for more than 20 years was a great physical and mental test for me. Since I came to CNOOD, my potential vigor has been kindled, and now I enjoy pushing the frontiers and working with young people to charge ahead.

I have nice experience in every aspect as I work with young people every day. The young CNOODers are neither arrogant nor impetuous and show respect for me, and I care for them with a loving heart. Many colleagues privately call me "Old Urchin." All in all, the working atmosphere is good and simple, with virtually no conflict. We share resources

如果说2020年刚到施璐德时是为促进业务开展，接下来我更希望在搭建新生代人才梯队方面贡献更多价值和力量。

一家企业想要持续发展，不断壮大，只靠一辈人是不行的。从商者会谈产业链，企业经营则需要人才链。不讲什么长江后浪推前浪，我们更注重推动每一位年轻人躬身入局。就如徐克导演曾说，入了江湖才算是江湖人，不入江湖最多只是个说书人。年轻人的战斗力提升，才能更好地实现团队作战的概念。年轻人在这个平台上，才有心力怀揣梦想，有能力实现愿景。

做项目怕的是缺经验，难的是没资源，这些需要靠时间积累，确实不能操之过急，但是否有加速的方法呢？答案是肯定的。我们这些具备职场经验和资源的老将就是。我们的贡献之一就是帮助大家如建立一个可持续发展的网络。

2008年开始，施璐德基本上都在经

and devote ourselves to fulfilling the tasks. Of course, this is inseparable from the corporate culture of CNOOD.

If it was my task to promote the business when I joined CNOOD in 2020, now I hope to make greater contributions in developing a tiered structure of talented people of the new generation.

A company cannot rely on only one generation of people if it wants to keep growing and become stronger. While businessmen talk about industrial chains, the management of a company requires talents chains. Instead of talking about "the new generation will invariably surpass the old," we pay more attention to encouraging every young member to be actively involved. As the film director Hark Tsui said, "You are a member of the wild world only if you are in it, otherwise you're no more than a storyteller." We can better realize the idea of "team battle" if young people's capabilities are enhanced. It is on this platform that young people are able to embrace a dream and realize it.

What we fear in doing projects is the lack of experience, and the main difficulty is the absence of resources. It takes time to accumulate experience or resources, and we cannot act hastily. But are there ways to accelerate the process? The answer is yes; one of the ways lies in the veterans like us, with workplace experience and resources. One of our contributions is to help people build a sustainable network.

Since 2008, CNOOD has primarily

营海外业务，如路桥设备、风电等。与国内不同，在海外，资源都需要一点一点推进，从一家到几家，从几家到几十家，都说从零到一是最难的，而这最难的一步，先遣队已经顺利达成。如今需要我们做的是稳中求发展，维系好当下的客户，再不断拓展。

打磨年轻人从沟通开始，没有人脉，我先负责链接，这之后就交给他们来沟通跟进，这个过程就考验他们的能力和耐力了。生意中会遇到形形色色的客户，机会在面前，如何把握要仔细思忖。想做有效沟通不是简单的事，要清楚自己有什么牌，我们的能力半径究竟在哪里，哪些能

been working on overseas businesses, such as road and bridge equipment, wind power projects, etc. Working overseas is different. We need to accumulate the resources bit by bit, from one client to several clients, and then dozens of them. The step from zero to one, which is believed to be the toughest one, has been successfully accomplished by our advance team. What we need to do now is to seek development in stability, retain our clients, and keep expanding our business.

The training of young people starts with communication. When they lack personal connections, I will pool the resources before letting them do the job of communication and follow-up. This process is a test of their skills and endurance. When doing business we

做，哪些绝对不能做，哪些跳一跳够得着，该怎么跳上去。意识要跟得上，思路要跟得上，最后磨炼的就是实操能力。这样几轮下来，想不成长都难。

在施璐德，建立人才梯队的方式不是筛选而是培养。公司很少淘汰员工，如果某一个领域不适合，那就换个领域重新开始。年轻人原本就风华正茂，各有各的特长，能够充分识别并善用他们的优势比淘汰更重要。

我们在做的项目，每一个从中标到交付都需要投入大量的时间和精力，如果团队不能做有效平衡和匹配，失去的不仅是订单，更是口碑和合作机遇。没有淘汰，不代表没有选择的标准，施璐德人最重要的特质就是快速反应，能"打硬仗"。委派下去的任务，只要我讲出一点，他们就会做到二三点，不需要把每个步骤都讲清楚，大家就知道该怎么做。这样的快速反应能力，就像一支机动部队，在打仗期间是很好用的。

will come across all kinds of clients; with opportunities in front of us, we must think carefully about how we can seize them. It is not an easy thing to carry out effective communication, and we must be clear about what cards we have, what we are capable of doing, what are the things we can do, what are the things we are absolutely forbidden to do, what are the goals we can achieve with an effort, and how we should make the effort. We must be well prepared in terms of awareness and ideas; in the end, it is the operational skills that will be sharpened. After a few rounds like this, growth is a sure thing.

At CNOOD, we develop a tiered structure of talented people not by screening, but by training. The approach of "elimination" is rarely used by the company. If a certain area is unsuitable for you, you just start over in another one. It is more important to fully identify and use the strengths of the young people, who are in the prime of life with their fortes, than to eliminate them.

Each of the projects we are working on requires a lot of time and energy, from winning the bid to delivery. If the team failed to achieve effective balance and matching, what we lose is not only the orders, but also reputation and cooperation opportunities. No elimination does not mean that there are no selection criteria. The most important trait of a CNOODer is the ability to respond rapidly and to "fight tough battles". For any task assigned to

当然,我们在业务方面也有相应的考核标准。比如我们采购中心,绩效考核条例都是相对完善的,基础岗位职能部分就通过规范来考核,但更重要的是靠"战场"上的应变力来做调整,所以要充分发挥团队的作用。

除此之外,我认为年轻人工作之余,也要增加对生活的体验。工作只是一种视角,生活会给予更广阔的空间。

4. 严以修身,重在三修

很多人知道我喜欢书法,现在每到年末,我都会写上百"福"字传递新春祝福,送给同事,送给朋友,还会送给客户和供应商。礼轻情意重,按现在的潮流,礼物要用 DIY 的更能表达心意和诚意。

them, so long as I point out one thing, they will proceed to do the next two or three things. There's no need to explain the details of the steps because everyone is perfectly clear about them. With such rapid responses, we are like a mobile force which is very useful during a battle.

Of course, we also have criteria for performance review in terms of business. In the Purchasing Center with relatively complete rules of performance review, the basic functions will be assessed according to the rules. More importantly, however, we rely on the "battlefield" adaptability to make adjustments. Therefore, we must give full play to the role of teams.

In addition, I believe that young people should also taste more of life after work. The work provides you with only one perspective, while life will give you broader space.

IV. The Three-Fold Self-Cultivation

Many of you know that I love calligraphy. At the end of every lunar year, I will write more than one hundred pieces of the character "福" (Fu, meaning "happiness") to send the best wishes to my

其实最早在接触书法时，它并不能算是我的爱好，而是小孩子必修的技能。我父亲字写得好，家里三兄弟，我是老大，父亲对我的要求更严格一些。他认为一个人的字是门面，字写得好的人，别人都会高看三分。所以在他的指导下，每天作业后我就开始练毛笔字。因为谈不上是兴趣，所以在掌握了一些基本功后，就没有再坚持一日一练，但因为写书法带来的好处，在后期求学和工作中还是会体现出来。

我们那时候没有初中、高中的划分，统一叫作中学。中学里会有一个负责全校宣传工作的学生团体，我也是其中一员。宣传工作包括发布通讯、写大幅宣传标语、每周五出学校黑板报。每个班级都配有一位通讯员，任务是每周收集本班的新人新事等，因为我写字还不错，所以这些宣传工作都由我承包了。现在看来，毛笔字虽然没有刻意练习和精进，但有宣传工作的经历，也相当于巩固了书法基础，并没有荒废。后来大学期间也断断续续练了一些。开始工作后，练字算是彻底搁置在一边，直到近五年，才又重新捡起来。

colleagues, friends, and also our clients and suppliers. As the saying goes, "It's a small gift, but it's the thought that counts." Or, according to the current trend, we can better express our goodwill and sincerity by a DIY gift.

In fact, when I was initiated into the art of calligraphy, it was not considered a hobby of mine, but rather a required skill for children. I was the oldest of the three sons in my family. My father, who was quite good at calligraphy, believed that one's handwriting was as important as one's appearance and that people would look up to someone who could write Chinese characters very well. With his guidance, I started to practice calligraphy after my homework. I could hardly say that I was interested in it, so I didn't keep practicing every day after I learned some basic skills. Nevertheless, the benefits brought by good handwriting were later reflected, in my school years and my career.

Time was when there were no "junior high schools" or "senior high schools" but only "high schools." There was a student group in our school responsible for school-wide publicity, and I was a member of it. We were responsible for newsletters, big banners with slogans on them, and the school blackboard newspaper published every Friday. Each class was assigned a correspondent, who collected materials about the "new persons and new things" in the class every week. With good handwriting skills, I took on every piece of the publicity work. When I look

这一次再练字，心境完全不同，有岁月的加持，有思想的转变，有需求的延伸，练字就成为我生活里不可或缺的一部分，每每提笔也更愉悦。所以，万事别急，沉淀在人生中的某些事物在合适的时机又会再次出现，而且会以更好的方式回归。

除了放松休闲，现在也偶尔会约上三五好友一起交流书画艺术。后经友人推荐，我加入上海市宝山书法家协会，同时拜入书法家郑小云先生门下，成为入室弟子。入会的目的也是想有个契机鞭策自己，既然重新拿起笔，就认真练习，作为书法家协会的一分子，字总要似模似样、说得过去才行。

back now, I didn't give up practicing calligraphy completely during my school days; my experience with the publicity work helped me solidify the foundation even though I didn't take great pains to practice and improve my skills of writing with an ink brush. Later, during my college years I practiced it intermittently, and after I started my career, it was suspended for a long time until I picked it up again about five years ago.

This time when I picked up calligraphy again, I was in a completely different state of mind. With the elapse of time, the changes of ideas, and the extension of needs, the practicing of calligraphy has become an indispensable part of my life, and it becomes even more enjoyable every time I put the ink brush to the paper. So, don't be in a hurry; some of the things that have settled in your life will emerge again at the right time, and in a better form.

Apart from having a relaxing time, I will occasionally meet several good friends to exchange views on calligraphy and Chinese painting. Introduced by my friends, I became a member of Calligraphers Association of Baoshan District, Shanghai City. I also became a pupil of Mr. Zheng Xiaoyun, a famous calligrapher. I joined the association to spur me on to take the practicing seriously since I have picked up the ink brush again. After all, I must attain a satisfactory level in calligraphy as a member of a calligraphers association.

现在每到春节这种传统节日，各类书法活动应接不暇。进入施璐德后，春节要写的字就更多了，有些供不应求的感觉，最多一次写了三百多幅"福"字，每年来我老丁这里讨一幅字，成为大家的乐趣，增添了新年仪式感，让关系和氛围更融洽。以真诚之心待之，也将收获真诚，何乐而不为。

如今，书法已经成为我的爱好之一，我愿意坚持不辍，也借此修心、修性、修行，三修渡己身。王阳明先生提出"事上磨，致良知"。经事来修，顿悟力会更强。

现在很多"80后""90后"喜欢谈天赋、讲悟性，也会花很长时间去寻找自己的天赋。在这个过程中，大部分人会产生内耗。

天才是存在的。有的人在某些方面的能力天生就比其他人强，我们不得不承认天赋确实起到重要的作用。就像我们读书的时候，有人拼命学，时间投入比其他人多得多，成绩却没那么好，而有的学生

I will attend a lot of calligraphy activities on every traditional Chinese festival, including the Spring Festival. Since I joined CNOOD, the task has become heavier, and I feel a little overwhelmed. There was an occasion where I wrote more than three hundred pieces of "福" at one time! It has become a pleasure for everyone to ask for a work of calligraphy from me every year. Adding to the festive atmosphere of the lunar New Year, it helps create a better workplace by shaping harmonious interpersonal relationships. Why should I not do it, when I'm replied with sincerity if I deal with people with a sincere heart?

Now calligraphy has become one of my hobbies, and I am willing to persist in it and to use it to cultivate my heart, my nature, and my practice. The three-fold self-cultivation is also a tool of self-salvation. Wang Yangming advanced the idea of "obtaining innate knowledge by practical exercise." If you cultivate yourself by practical exercise, you would have stronger insights.

Many people of the post-80s or post-90s generation like to talk about talent and enlightenment, who spend a lot of time in seeking their own talent. In this process, most of them will experience internal burnout.

Genius does exist. Some people are born with a stronger ability in certain area than others, for which we have to admit the important roles of talent. When we were at school, some students worked

只上上课、写写作业，就能轻松考到前几名。与其说这与智商有关，不如说与天生的悟性有关。

说到这，可能有人会焦虑，好处都让天才占了，拔尖的事情都让天才做了，那我们普通人怎么办？

我小时候，国家提倡的一句口号是"增强人民体质"。为了响应国家号召，我们都会选择一项感兴趣的体育运动。大家如果看过电影《中国乒乓之绝地反击》就会大致了解，那个年代乒乓球是普及的，我和身边的很多同学都选了乒乓球来练习。当时条件并不好，日常运动的场所就是小区中间架起一块与乒乓球桌相同尺寸的水泥板，中间用砖头做拦网。

乒乓球很锻炼人的反应力、思考力和耐力，想练好不容易。那时候的人做事更认真，只要锚定一件事，就要打出点成绩，打出点名堂。这也是我一直以来的行事准则，把功夫放在日常，把劲头用在提升。后来我开始在学校比赛和一些其他赛事中获得比较好的名次。任何事情困难再大，只要你尽最大的努力做到坚持，即使失败也继续努力，遇到的问题就都不是问题。

very hard and put in much more time than others, but didn't do very well in terms of academic achievements, while some students were at the top of the class in exams by just attending the class and doing the homework. This is not so much related to IQ, but rather correlated with innate enlightenment.

Then someone may be anxious: with geniuses taking advantage of all the favorable conditions and excelling at all things, what is there left for us to do?

When I was a child, the nation calls for "building up people's health." Answering this call, everyone would choose a sport that interested him/her. If you have seen the movie *Ping Pong: The Triumph*, you will have a general idea of the popularity of table tennis in those days. Many of my classmates and I chose table tennis. We didn't have very good conditions for sport, and the place for daily exercise was a concrete board the size of a table-tennis table set in the center of the neighborhood, lined by bricks in the middle as the net.

Table tennis is a good sport to improve one's reflexes, thinking power, and endurance, and it's not easy to be good at it. At that time, people were more serious in what they did; they won't stop until they make some achievement in what they're determined to do. This is also the principle that I have been guided by in all these years: devoting efforts in daily routine and enthusiasm in self-cultivation. Later, I started to get a better

金字塔顶端我们无法跻身，其他层级总是可以达成的。更多时候，外人看到的游刃有余，都是当事人日复一日"事上磨"达成的。

　　不是天才，没有天赋怎么办？努力和刻苦就是答案。小时候我常听的一句话"笨鸟先飞"，放到当下依然可用。我也是一个自小没什么天赋的人，因为及早认清这一点，所以比其他人付出得更多一些。

　　流水不争先，争的是滔滔不绝。当你投入大量的时间精力去坚持一件事情，总会水到渠成。也许最后收获的不是当初预期的结果，但我相信一定比你的预期更精彩。

　　最后，在年度交汇之际，要感谢2022年，一个在历史时间线上平凡普通，但在人类历史上极具意义的一年。这一年，施璐德人同心协力经受住了各类突发事件的考验，居于时代潮头。2023年，愿我们继往开来，所向披靡！

ranking in school competitions and some other events. Whatever difficulties you may face, you can overcome them if you do your best relentlessly and continue to work hard even if you fail.

We can't get to the top of the social ladder, but we can always reach other lower stages. The skills and ease you display is often the result of your repeated "practical exercise" day after day.

What if you are not a genius or a person with talent? I believe that the answer lies in hard work and diligence. An old saying which I often heard when I was a child, "The clumsy birds have to start flying early", is still applicable at present. I'm a person with little talent since childhood, who, having a sober awareness of this fact, has made more efforts than others.

The flowing water does not compete for being the first, but for being sustainable. When you invest a large amount of time and energy in doing one thing, success will be assured one day. Perhaps the result you get in the end is not what you originally expected, but I believe it will be a better one.

Finally, at the turn of the year I would like to express my gratitude for 2022, an ordinary year in the historical timeline, and yet a year of great significance in human history. Working hard together, CNOODers stood the test of various unexpected shocks, staying at the forefront of the times. In 2023, may we continue to forge ahead and always be invincible!

丁征宇
Zhengyu Ding

1960年5月出生，浙江绍兴人，毕业于现名为上海应用技术大学钢铁冶金专业。1994—2020年就职于德国蒂森克虏伯公司，2020年5月退休；同年7月加入施璐德亚洲有限公司。工作认真、做事靠谱，正直善良、热爱生活，乐于助人、善于交友，喜欢书法和运动。

Born in May 1960 in Shaoxing, Zhejiang Province, Zhengyu graduated from now named Shanghai Institute of Technology majoring in Steel Metallurgy. He worked in thyssenkrupp from 1994 to 2020 and retired in May 2020. In July of the same year, he joined CNOOD ASIA LIMITED. A reliable and hardworking man, he is best known for his integrity, kindness, and his love for life. He is ready to help anyone in need, while good at making friends. His hobbies include calligraphy and sports.

迎潮而上，顺势而为

Ride the Tide, and Seize the Momentum

■ Lin Zhang

写这篇文章的时候，我刚好工作了40个年头，年满60，可以为职场人生画句号、开启退休逍遥游了。但现在看来，句号还不太好画，主要是我自己目前还没有这方面的打算。

这个社会变化很快，这几十年说是天翻地覆也不为过。不像我的父母辈，他们在退休之前经历的年代，生活和工作的方式变化都不大。如果你当时大学毕业了，基本上可以什么都不用再学，学校里学的东西差不多就够用一辈子了。

但是我参加工作的40年，学止于大学就完全不够了。尤其是现在，稍微一个懈怠，我就有点跟不上步伐。不管是工作知识方面，还是生活常识方面，甚至是观

By the time I write this essay, I have worked for forty years and, at the age of sixty, have reached a stage where I can put a full stop to my career and start my post-retirement life of leisure. But now it seems that I'm not ready to put that full stop, largely because I do not have a plan of doing so.

The past few decades have witnessed radical or even earth-shaking — if we might use the word — changes in our society. Things were different in the years before my parents retired, when the way of life and work did not change much. If you graduated from college at that time, you didn't have to learn anything new afterward because what you had learned in college was basically enough for you in the rest of your life.

During the forty years of my career, however, it would have been far from enough if I had stopped learning the moment I graduated from college. In

念，每时每刻都在变化，稍不留神年轻人在说什么话我可能都听不懂。

这四十年的变化确实非常大，我们被时代洪流推动，很少有机会坐下来想一想。如今写这篇文章，刚好借此机会回顾盘点这四十年。这么多年，在遇到一些转折时，我也只是顺势而为，做事是认真做，但只局限于做好一件事情，在事上琢磨，从没想过人生的远大理想。

1. 家风沐浴求学路

我生于小城泰县（现江苏省泰州市姜堰区），父亲是一位厨师，母亲是服装厂的工人。父亲早年间读过几年私塾，认识一些字，后因家中生活压力大，14岁就出来做学徒。母亲从小没读过书，但本分老实、吃苦耐劳。我们家中有三个孩子，哥哥、姐姐和我。那个时代养孩子，吃饱穿暖就是万岁。

present-day society, I would not be able to keep up even with the slightest slackness. Changes are taking place at every moment in terms of professional expertise, general knowledge of life, or even people's ideas. I might fail to understand what young people are saying if I don't pay enough attention.

With the tremendous changes in the past forty years, we have all been pushed by the powerful tide of the times and hardly had the chance to sit down and think for a while. Now that I am writing this essay, I would like to take this opportunity to review the past forty years. During these years, when I encountered some twists and turns, what I did was just to seize the momentum. I was serious about what I worked on, but I never thought about the lofty ideals of life, concentrating my efforts on doing things right.

I. The Journey of My Studies and the Family Tradition

I was born in Taixian, a small county in Jiangsu Province (now Jiangyan District, Taizhou City). My father was a cook and my mother worked in a clothing factory. When he was a child, my father attended an old-style tutorial school for a few years and obtained a rudimentary knowledge of Chinese characters. Because of the pressure on livelihood at home, he became an apprentice at the age of fourteen. My mother, though never having the chance of going to school, was an honest, decent, and hardworking

父母平时都要工作，没什么时间和精力管我们，哥哥姐姐陆续上学后，家中无人再看管我。所以在我6周岁不到的时候，他们就商量把我送去学校，但因为我的生日是下半年，实际年龄还不够入学标准，长得也瘦瘦小小，完全不像个小学生，学校老师搬出规章制度婉拒了我的入学申请。无奈之下，父亲找到另外一个县城郊区的学校，校长是父亲一位同事的家属。那所学校教学质量不太高，制度也并不严格，校长说，只要墙上这几个字你能认得，我就收下你。幸好父亲教我识得一些汉字，加之"毛主席万岁"那几个大字在当时处处可见，所以我流畅地读了出来。

就这样，托毛主席的福，我开启了小学生活。我们那时候没有小升初考试，也没有中考，都是就近制度，家住哪里就选

person. There were three children in our family: my elder brother, my elder sister, and me. In those days, it was more than satisfactory if a family had enough food and clothes for their children.

Busy with their daily work, my parents hardly had the time for the three children. When my elder brother and sister went to school, there was no one left to take care of me at home. So my parents decided to send me to school before I reached the age of six. But because my birthday was in the second half of the year, I hadn't reached the legal age for attending an elementary school. Besides, I didn't look like a schoolboy at all because of my small and thin stature. The schoolteacher politely rejected my application, citing the rules and regulations. In desperation, my father and I paid a visit to a school located in the suburbs of another county, whose principal was a family member of one of my father's colleagues. Its quality of teaching was not so satisfactory, while rules and regulations were not very strict. "As long as you can read these words on the wall," said the principal, "I will accept you." Fortunately, my father had taught me quite a few Chinese characters, and the characters on the wall, LONG LIVE CHAIRMAN MAO, could be seen everywhere in those days. I read them aloud fluently.

This was how I started my life in elementary school, thanks to Chairman Mao. In those days, we did not have

择附近的学校就读。初中毕业后，我就回到了所住县城里的高中——姜堰中学，父亲就在这个学校做后勤工作。在没有电视的年代，这所高中在全国都很出名，全因它极高的升学率。可想而知，这所学校的教学制度比较严格，教学质量也比较高。

我是 1979 届毕业生，刚好是高考恢复之后第三年，题目出得异常刁钻，这就对那些平时靠死记硬背考高分的学生不太友好，背的都不考，考的都不会。这恰好让我沾了点光，因为我平时学习不算用功，属于脑子比较灵光但不勤奋的那一类，所以那一年虽然分数不高，但也不差。

高考成绩出来后，我进入华东水利学院，也就是现在的河海大学，专业是港口与航道工程。为什么选这个专业呢？是因为班主任看到专业里面有"港口"两个字，班主任说，有港口的一定是海边的城市，将来的工作条件会好一些，就报这个

senior or junior high school entrance examinations, under a system of "neighborhood school" — all children went to the schools near their homes. After graduating from junior high school, I went back to my native county town and attended Jiangyan High School there, while my father worked in the logistics department of that school. The school had a nation-wide reputation for its extremely high rate of admission to colleges in an era when there was no television, so you can imagine its strict way of teaching and its high quality of education.

I graduated from senior high school in 1979, the third year since the resumption of the National University Entrance Examination. The questions in that year's examination were unusually tricky, not very friendly to those students who had relied on rote memory to get high scores: what they had memorized were not tested, while what were tested were beyond their ability. I was lucky enough to benefit from the situation, for I was not very diligent in my studies, belonging to the clever-but-not-hardworking type, so my performance in the examination were not bad, though not very good either.

After the results of the examination were published, I was admitted to East China Institute of Water Resources (now Hohai University), majoring in port and waterway engineering. Why did I choose this major? It was because my class

专业。现在回想起来还觉得很有趣，一个敢断，一个敢信。我走的每一步似乎都是顺势而为，并未费什么心思。

teacher, seeing the word "port" in the name of the major, convinced me that the job location must be in a coastal city and the future working conditions there would be better for me. When I recall the anecdote now, I am still amused by my class teacher's confidence as well as my boldness. It seemed that I just seized the momentum in every step I took, without taking the trouble to think hard.

在早期求学阶段，对我影响最大也最深远的就是家风。《南史》中有"各禀家风"的说法，我自小所受的便是父母的言传身教，这是我们三兄妹成长的精神足印。

家风之一是诚实。父母亲从来不撒谎，他们绝对不会去做不诚信的事，这也影响到我们。如果现在让我去做一些略带欺骗的事，我的内心会非常恐慌。

家风之二是自强。在我的印象中，父亲一直早出晚归、沉默寡言。他每天早晨5点起床，先做好早饭，没等我们醒来就去上班了，晚上入睡时，他还没回来，想见他只能等到放假。小时候他最常带我做的事就是写字。父亲虽然没读几年书，但字写得工整得体，我们学校的老师都很惊讶，一个厨师居然写得一手好毛笔字。父亲带我认字、写字大多用糯米面。我们每年都要晒糯米面，先把面均匀洒在竹匾上，再用河蚌壳刮平，父亲就用筷子在上面写字，我也跟着学，写满了再抹平，反反复复。

During my early school years, it was the family tradition that exerted the biggest and most profound influence on me. In *History of the Southern Dynasties*, there is an expression "each following his family tradition," and my parents have taught me by words and deeds since I was a little child. This is the mental footprints followed by our three siblings.

One feature of the family traditions is honesty. My parents never lied and would never do anything dishonest. We have all been influenced by them. I will be filled with fear if I'm asked to do something even slightly deceiving.

Another feature of the family tradition is the willpower to become stronger. As far as I can remember, my father was an uncommunicative person and always went out early in the morning and came home late in the evening. He got up at five o'clock every morning and made breakfast for the family. Usually going to work before we woke up and coming back home when I was already asleep, he could hardly be seen unless on holidays. When I was a child, one thing he took me to do most frequently was to practice calligraphy. Although he hadn't received much formal education, my father had very neat handwriting, and the teachers at my school were amazed that a cook could write Chinese characters so skillfully. My father instructed me to read and write, mostly with flour. When every year we dried glutinous rice flour in the sun, we started with sprinkling the flour evenly in

父亲对我们的学习期望很高,但从来不讲,如果我们考试成绩不好,他的失望会写在脸上。父亲一直是自强的人,他觉得尽管自己只是一名厨师,但子女不会比老师的子女差,大家都是一样的。所以,在我们三个孩子的学习上,父亲是暗自铆足了劲儿的。我们也算没有辜负他的培养,先后考上大学,全部出去读书。孩子争气,最自豪的就是父母,于他们而言也就没有任何遗憾了。在他们那代人的意识里,日子过得再紧也没关系,孩子就是最大的骄傲,父亲不会因为自己是一个普通的工人或者母亲斗大字不识而自卑、自损,反而极为勤奋,很珍惜自己的口碑,只要是他经手的事,几乎没有人说不好,这是做人做事的态度。每次有人说,这菜一定是张师傅做的,别人做不出来,他就开心得不得了。虽然他只是一位厨师,但在我们那里也算小有名气,一般人家有红白喜事,都会请他去家里掌厨,他就夹着一把厨刀和一件围裙过去了。报酬可能就是一条烟,但这份认可对他来说很重要。

a big, round, and shallow bamboo basket, and then scraped it with a clamshell to form a smooth surface, on which my father wrote characters with a chopstick. Then I would copy him repeatedly, smoothing it out when the surface was full of characters.

My father had high expectations of our academic performance at school, but never talked about it. His disappointment would be all on his face if we did not do well in exams. As a person always striving to be stronger, my father believed that his children would not be any worse than the children of schoolteachers, even though he was only a cook. So he did his best as regards the education of the three children. We lived up to his expectations and left our hometown to study at colleges one after another. Being most proud of their children's success, my parents didn't have regrets anymore. For people from their generation, children were their greatest pride, even if they had to struggle with financial straits. My father would not be self-abased because he was just an ordinary worker or his wife was virtually illiterate. On the contrary, he was extremely diligent and cherished his reputation very much. No one would be dissatisfied with anything my father did, reflecting his attitude of doing things. He would be thrilled every time someone commented, "This dish must have been cooked by Master Zhang; no one else can do it." Though only a cook, he became somewhat famous in the hometown.

父母的言传身教对我们的影响确实非常大，现在我 60 岁了，老母亲偶尔还会耳提面命："我们都百年之后，你们不能散了，你们还是兄弟姊妹，不要有矛盾，不要吵架。"我说："你放心吧，都是你带出来的孩子，不可能的。"

近几年，家风这个概念被越来越多地提起，对我们这代人来说，家风不是概念，不是说出来的，而是实实在在的践行和传承。

2. 止于浪漫，始于港口

那时候大学毕业有国家分配，国家让去哪里工作就去哪里，在 1983 年我大四快毕业时，国家提出了一个新需求——要提高部队基层指挥官的文化素质。

当时中国部队的基层指挥官，排长、连长，甚至团长，文化水平较低，不能够适应军队改革和现代化发展的需要。国家

Whenever there was a wedding or funeral banquet, he would be invited to be the head cook. Then he would happily go with a kitchen knife and an apron. The reward might just be a carton of cigarettes, but people's recognition meant a lot to him.

The influence of our parents' teaching by words and deeds was indeed profound. Now I'm sixty years old, and my mother still occasionally give me earnest instructions: "After we die, the three of you must not split up. Remember you are brothers and sisters, and don't fall out with each other." And I will reply, "Don't worry, that wouldn't happen with children brought up by you."

In recent years, the idea of family tradition has been discussed more and more. For our generation, family tradition is not a concept, not something that is spoken, but something that is practiced and passed on in a concrete way.

II. The End of a Romance and a Journey Starting with a Port

At that time, every college graduate was assigned a job by the government, and you could only work wherever you were told to go. When I was about to graduate, there was a new demand by the government—to improve the education level of junior commanding officers in the military.

At that time, junior commanding officers in Chinese troops, including platoon commanders, company

决定从大学应届毕业生当中招募基层指挥官,由学校内部先进行选拔,把名单报给部队来的首长,体检通过后进入部队的指挥官学校再读一年,出来就任排长。刚毕业的大学生有机会进入部队,进修后还能直接当军官,这样的机会何其宝贵。

我们这一届三个班总计一百多人,一共有三个名额,其中就有我一个。当时不知道是从哪里听到的消息,说很大可能是去海军所属的部队,那种开心和自豪就更加强烈了:望碧波之浩淼,看巨浪之排空;驭大轮以挺进,向深蓝而从容。依稀都能想象到自己未来站在指挥舰上与蓝天大海为伴的样子。

可部队首长来带兵时,我才发现美梦做得早了,不是海军,是炮兵。当时我对炮兵的粗浅理解是:打仗都见不到对方,搞不好人家一炮就把我干掉了,这样的未来太不浪漫了。失望渐起,我在主观上已

commanders, and even regimental commanders, were generally not well educated, who were not able to adapt to the needs of army reform and modern development. The government then decided to recruit junior commanding officers from among college graduates. The candidates went through an internal selection procedure, and their names and information were reported to the head officers in the military. After passing physical examination, they would study at the military academy for one year before they became platoon commanders. The opportunity to join the army and to become an officer directly after training was invaluable for college graduates.

Only three students in the three classes with more than a hundred students could have the chance. Fortunately, I was one of them. I didn't know where I heard the news that it was very likely for us to serve in the navy. Then my joyousness and pride became even keener, believing that I would soon be able to "gaze at the waves of the vastness, and see the billows soar aloft," and "steer the gigantic ship to advance, facing the deep blue ocean with calm." I couldn't wait to imagine myself standing on the command ship in the future, with the blue sky and sea as my companions.

But when the head officers from the military came for recruitment, I realized that I had my fond dream too soon: it was not the navy, but the artillery. At that time, I only had a superficial

经开始打退堂鼓，但既然已经报了名，得到学校推荐，即使有些不情愿，我肯定也会按照要求和流程继续进行。

就在这时，班上一位广东湛江来的同学私下跟我商量，基于国家分配政策，他毕业后就要回到湛江，那时湛江还相对闭塞，他既然考了大学走出来就不想再回去。而我如果不去部队，分配工作的地点大概率就是南京或上海，前景会好一些。他希望我去跟老师申请，主动放弃从军名额，这样他就有机会入选。我想了想，既然自己主观上并没那么想去，同学又有迫切需求，何不成人之美。

我找到老师，表示自己坚持要退出选拔，老师没有办法只能尊重我的决定，找到那位同学把我的名额顶上。虽然有了参选机会，但听说他后来体检没通过，失去了进入部队的机会。这件事对我来说影响其实并不大，但老师却一直记得，多年后再见面还耿耿于怀，不理解我为什么在关

understanding of the artillery: I could not even see my opponent in the battle and might be finished off with one shot. This was far from being romantic. Disappointment was building up, and I was already considering backing out. But since I had already entered for it and been recommended by the college, I would definitely go through the procedure as required even if I was somewhat reluctant.

Then one of my classmates who was from Zhanjiang, Guangdong Province, came to discuss with me in private. According to the national policy, he had to return to his hometown after graduation. At that time, Zhanjiang was still an out-of-the-way place, and he did not want to go back since he had left it. On the other hand, if I didn't join the army, it was most likely that I would be assigned to work in Nanjing or Shanghai, with a better future for my career. He wanted me to talk to the teacher and voluntarily give up the opportunity to join the army so that he would have a chance to be selected. I thought about it: since I didn't want to go that much, and my classmate was in an urgent need, why not help him fulfill his wish?

I called on my teacher and insisted on withdrawing from the selection. The teacher had no choice but to respect my decision and gave the chance to my classmate. However, I heard later that he didn't pass the physical examination and failed to join the army. My teacher always

键时刻放弃了。

人生的选择有时候很奇妙，就像扔硬币，正面或背面朝上的概率是相同的，我们也很难在当下那一刻就知道自己的选择究竟是对还是错，大部分人都认为妥当的事，也不一定就是完美的。在毕业之初看，进入部队也许是全局最优解，但从长远看，那也许只能算是一个局部最优解。

放弃了进入部队的名额，毕业后我被分配到江苏连云港，也就是江苏最北边的一个小城市。那时候的连云港偏僻且落后，公共交通设施都还不完善，有种回到了小村镇的即视感。虽然环境差了一些，但我入职的单位是中交建，资深央企，隶属于国家交通部的施工单位，各项福利待遇都很好。我拿到了人生中第一张工作证，上面写着：中华人民共和国交通运输部。看到这个名头就知道公司在当地名气很大。

我毕业工作那年是改革开放第五年，正是全国港口建设的新时期，连云港也面临着扩大建港，一切都在建设发展阶段，也是人力物力急需的时期。我从 1983 年

remembered this incident, which actually exerted little impact on my life, and nagged about it when we met again many years later, wondering why I gave up at the critical moment.

Life choice is sometimes amazing. It's like tossing a coin: the probability of heads or tails facing up is the same, and it's hard to know in the moment whether our choice is right. What most people think is right is not necessarily perfect. At the moment I graduated from college, joining the army might seem to be the global optimal solution; when seen from the long-run perspective, it may only be a local optimal solution.

After I gave up the opportunity to join the army, I was assigned to work in Lianyungang in the northernmost part of Jiangsu Province. It was a remote and economically backward small city at that time, with unsatisfactory public transportation facilities, and looked like a rural place. Despite the environment, I worked for China Communications Construction Group, a construction company under the Ministry of Transport with superb welfare. I got the first employee's card in my life, with the words "Ministry of Transport of the People's Republic of China" on it. Seeing this you'll know how famous the company was in the city.

The year I graduated from college was exactly the fifth year since the adoption of the policy of reform and opening up. It was a new period for

一直工作到2002年，接近二十年的时间，这期间有一多半不在连云港。工程人的特质就是到处跑，项目在哪里就往哪里去。我也成为公司里第一个带团队到本土以外的地方去组织工程项目的人。春节档有部热映电影叫《流浪地球》，20世纪80年代末开始，我们这一批工程人也逐渐挂上了流浪探索的属性，1992年去深圳，1995年去缅甸，1997年香港地区回归之后才再次回到连云港。

port construction across the country and Lianyungang was also about to expand its port. Everything was in the stage of rapid development. It was also a period when human and material resources were badly needed. I worked for nearly twenty years from 1983 to 2002, during which I was away from Lianyungang for more than half of the time. The characteristic of engineers people is to travel around and go wherever the project is. I became the first person in the company who led a team to carry out engineering projects outside the country. There was a hit movie during the Spring Festival, *The Wandering Earth*. Starting from the late

我是较早一批进入公司的，算是为集团在发展过程中开疆拓土尽了自己的绵薄之力，只要没有原则性错误，工作态度认真，能力也不差，很容易得到提拔。当时集团开始推荐在职员工返校就学，攻读工程管理硕士，于是1998年，我通过基础知识考试后顺利入学再深造。2000年，我36岁，集团提拔我进入公司管理层，成为公司副总经理兼任总工。

在同事和员工看来，我就算走上仕途了。一时间，周围充斥着各种声音，但对我来讲，我并没有一门心思要求取这些名头和职位，所以心态一直是平稳的，有些事情做着做着也就水到渠成了。

3. 迎潮头而上，顺势头而生

1998年开始，网络走进了大众视野，但并未完全普及，媒体资讯等还不能高速流通，身处国内，如果不是有意识探知，普通百姓并不知道海外发展如何。我那时每天的工作就是在工地研究方案，副总经

1980s, our team also became somehow "wandering," always on the way of exploring: going to Shenzhen in 1992 and Myanmar in 1995, before coming back to Lianyungang after the return of Hong Kong in 1997.

I was one of the earliest ones to join the company and did my part for the group in its development and expansion. So long as I didn't make mistakes in matters of principle, it was easy for me, with my diligence and ability, to get promoted. At that time, the group began to recommend serving employees to return to college for a master's degree in Engineering Management. In 1998, I passed the basic knowledge examination and successfully enrolled for further study. In 2000 when I was thirty-six years old, I was raised by the group to management level and became the deputy general manager and chief engineer.

In my colleagues' opinion, I had eventually embarked on the path of official career. For a while, I was surrounded by various gossips, but I didn't focus on seeking titles or positions. Therefore, I kept a steady mentality, believing that success would be assured with persistent efforts.

III. Born to Ride the Tide

From 1998 on, internet came into the public view but was not popularized, without a high-speed flow of media information. If you lived in China at that time, you would have no idea how things

理办公室的椅子基本没坐热过，总工的职能倒是游刃有余。一方面是因为我对工程始终秉持一个态度——现场有神灵，做工程脱离现场就像打仗远离战场；另一方面是因为在计划经济年代，安排我们做什么就做什么，还不流行人力资源管理和财务管理。

做出出国的决定，于我而言很简单，但听到这个消息的人都非常不理解。我离开的时候公司有近两千名员工，领导只有5人，领导千人团队的机会说放弃就放弃，在他们的观念里，我放弃的不只是工作，也是所谓成功人士的身份。人这一生，随着年龄增大，得到的越来越多，尝过了拥有的滋味，想要割舍就变得艰难，一旦要放弃点什么，随之而来的就是恐惧。对大多数人而言，放弃当下就意味着赖以生存的安全感消失了。但他们或许忘记了，自己本身才是那个创造者，就像计算机处理数据的基本单位0和1，看起来简单，但只要有这两个单位就能无限创造。中国有句俗语说得很好："留得青山在，不怕没柴烧。"

were going in other countries unless you consciously sought information about that. My daily work at that time was to study the working plans for engineering projects at the construction sites. I hardly had the time to sit in the deputy general manager's office, while I did my job perfectly well as the chief engineer. On one hand, I always held an attitude towards engineering projects that "there are gods in the site," and working on engineering projects away from the site was like fighting a battle away from the battlefield. On the other hand, we did what we were ordered to do in the era of planned economy, when the ideas of human resources management and financial management were not popular yet.

It was quite easy for me to make the decision of going abroad, a decision incomprehensible for people who heard the news. When I left the company, there were nearly two thousand employees, with only five persons at the management level. So I simply gave up the chance of leading a team of one thousand members. In their opinion, what I gave up was not only a job, but also the social status of the so-called "successful people." As we grow older and achieve more, it will be difficult for us to part with something once we have owned it; we will be filled with fear if we have to abandon something. For most people, giving up what they have now means the disappearance of the sense of security upon which their survival depends. They may have forgotten, however, that they themselves are *the* creators, just like the 0 and 1, the basic units by which a computer processes data. Simple as they may look, they are the very foundation for infinite creation. As the saying goes, "When there is life, there is hope."

4. 原来地球真的是圆的

《阿甘正传》里面说："人生就像一盒巧克力，你永远也不知道下一块是什么。"我和儿子在登上飞往加拿大的飞机时，也完全没预料过会遇到什么、经历什么。但命运就是会在最恰当的时候为你安排一个转机，这种不可思议被很多人称为奇迹，我把它叫作成事的心力。

飞机上，我和儿子一直在聊天。坐在我旁边的人来自中国台湾，他一直在默默关注我们，快下飞机时，总算听明白这对父子究竟去加拿大是要做什么，于是主动问我，到加拿大是否有亲人？是否有安排？是否有计划？在听到我连番说没有之后，他拿出了一张名片，表示我自己一个人带孩子落地开始新生活肯定不太容易，如果有困难需要工作，可以去这家公司，专业也许不一定对口，但至少可以帮我解决前期可能会遇到的困难。我对他的慷慨表示感谢，但心里并没有把这个当回事，随手就把名片揣在包里了。

IV. Indeed the Earth Is Round

There is a line in the movie *Forrest Gump*, "Life is like a box of chocolates, you never know what you're going to get." When my son and I got on board the plane for Canada, we didn't know what we were going to meet or experience. But fate would arrange for you a favorable turn at the best moment, an incredible thing that many people call "miracle." I prefer to call it "the willpower to make things happen."

My son and I kept talking during the flight, while a gentleman from Taiwan, China sitting beside us paid silent attention to us. When we were about to get off the plane, he finally understood what we were going to do in Canada. He then asked me whether I had any relatives in Canada and whether I had any arrangements or plans. Hearing my repeated answers of "No," he produced a business card and said, "It would not be easy for you to start a new life on your own with a child. If you have any difficulty and need a job, you may go and work at this company. The job might not necessarily match your expertise, but it

来到加拿大的第一天晚上，因为倒时差睡不着，我忽然意识到，地球果然是圆的。虽然前几年因公去过缅甸，但感觉那里的时间和中国没太大区别，可加拿大与国内时差有十几个小时，这才真正体会到什么是一个白天一个黑夜，曾经学过的地理知识得到实际验证，这样直观的感受让我觉得很新鲜。

2002年刚到加拿大时，正赶上全球发达国家就业形势下滑，我的语言又不算精通，找工作很难。所以我决定先去参加政府免费开办的英语补习班，另外就是要尽快找到房子，也要同步联系相关部门把儿子送到学校读书。

等一切尘埃落定已经过了一个月，我才想起飞机上那位台湾朋友给我的名片。我尝试拨电话过去沟通，对方说，我等了你快一个月，但你迟迟没有联系，原本办公室有一个技术类的岗位，因为你没来，所以刚刚定下了人，如果你愿意来，目前只能分配到仓库，职位类似于库管。来到

could at least help you solve the problems you might come across in the early stage." I thanked him for his generosity, but I didn't take this seriously and casually put the business card in my bag.

Because of the jet lag, I couldn't fall asleep the first night I was in Canada. Then it occurred to me, all of a sudden, that the earth is round indeed. Although I had been to Myanmar for business a few years before, I didn't find much difference there in terms of time. It was in Canada that I truly came to know what it was like to have day and night at the same time, with a time difference of more than ten hours between Canada and China. It was quite a strange thing for me that the geographical knowledge I had learned was verified directly by my personal experience.

When I arrived in Canada in 2002, it was difficult for me to find a job because the situation of employment in developed countries around the world was worsening and I was not proficient in English. So I decided to attend a free English tutorial class offered by the government, to find a house as soon as possible, and to contact the relevant authorities to send my son to school at the same time.

It was not until one month later when everything was settled that I remembered the business card given to me by the Taiwanese gentleman on the plane. I dialed the phone number on the card, and the voice at the other end of the line said, "I have waited for

新国家，身处新环境，生存是首位，况且我们当时的存款也并没有那么多，只能勉强维持一段时日，没有收入肯定是不行的，做库管是目前最好的选择。其实库管在国外薪资也很不错，比当时国内的工程师要高很多，平均一个小时可以拿到10到20美元，一天工作下来，大概有500元人民币。

打工之余，我除了精进语言学习，也在思考接下来的工作规划。库管只是暂时过渡，我自然是希望能从事和自己专业相关的工作，在加拿大继续做工程师。但就业形势不明朗，还没有太好的机会推进，而且在这里工作也需要获得当地政府认可的工程师就业资质，我要先到高校里去参加工程管理的短期学习来获取证书。在此期间，我结识了一部分短期班的同学，和大家积极交流就业机会。也在机缘巧合下得知，我曾经的同学、朋友也有移民到加拿大的，都在多伦多这座城市，大家又借此机会重新建立联系、增进沟通，新国家的人脉网络逐渐铺设起来。

you for almost a month, but you didn't contact me. Actually we had a technical position available in the office, but we've just found a person for the job since you didn't come earlier. Now if you are still willing to come, you can only be assigned to a position something like a warehouse keeper in China." Being in a new country and new environment, we must survive first. Without so much savings at that time, it was impossible for us to live in that country if I had no income at all. Being a warehouse keeper turned out to be my best choice then. In fact, the salary for such a job in western countries was not bad, much higher than that of engineers in China at that time; in average I earned 10 to 20 US dollars an hour, or approximately 500 RMB yuan a day.

In my spare time, I thought about my working plans for the next stage while refining my language skills. The warehouse keeper's job was only temporary, and I wanted to be an engineer in Canada, doing a job related to my expertise. However, the employment situation was uncertain, and there were not too many good opportunities, while I needed an employment qualification recognized by the local government to work there as an engineer and must take a short-term course in engineering management to obtain the certificate. During that period, I met some of my classmates in the short-term course and actively exchanged employment

放下工作不说，我很感谢有这样一个经历，在人生转折期可以有机会和儿子一起体验。太太还没出国前，每天就是我们两个人，相比过去忙碌的生活，我们多了互动和沟通。他会主动跟我讲学校的情况、学习的进展，而我在这个阶段也更多体会到为人父的责任和快乐，我们会一起从人生的角度讨论更深层次的内容。儿子小时候常说，我就想成为我爸那样的人！听到儿子的话，我就觉得身为父亲很自豪。

如今，儿子早已自学校毕业走入职场。总体来讲，我觉得他做得很好，刚到多伦多没多久，他就充分展示了自己的独立性，逐渐长大的过程中，他也懂得潜心修炼本领，自食其力，如果说现在我对他还有什么期待，就是希望他在工作和生活之余能够多看一些书，我年轻的时候没人告诉我应该看哪些书，一些哲学、历史、文学方面的书如果能在人生早期就有涉猎，会受益匪浅。另外，我希望他不要复制我，不要等到50岁才开始反思。"业精于勤荒于嬉，行成于思毁于随"，无论在

opportunities with them. I also learned by chance that some of my old classmates and friends had also immigrated to Canada and were all in the city of Toronto, so we took this opportunity to re-establish contact and communication, gradually building a network in this new country.

Putting the work aside, I am grateful for the experience of having the opportunity to be with my son during a transitional period in my life. Before my wife came to Canada, there were just the two of us every day. Compared to the busy lives in previous years, we now had more interactions and communication. He would tell me about the school life and the progress he made in his studies, and I experienced more strongly the responsibility and joy of being a father. We would discuss the deeper aspects of life together. When he was a little kid, my son would often say, "I want to be like my dad!" I felt proud to be a father every time I heard this.

My son has already graduated from college and started his career. In general, I think he has done a good job. Not long after he arrived in Toronto, he showed his full independence, and as he grew up, he knew how to concentrate on his skills and earn his own living. If there is anything else I expect from him, it is that I hope he will read more books in his spare time. When I was young, no one told me which books I should read. In fact, one will benefit a lot if he reads books on

什么年龄阶段，都要"勤于思，敏于行"，思考这辈子你想成为一个怎样的人，你想对这个社会有什么贡献，而不是只关注我今天吃了个牛排，明天又去滑了个雪，这些都是表面的，君子志存深远，不求一时之乐。

5. 清零不是归零，原点亦是起点

我接到了原单位同事的电话，他提及他们的集团会在巴拿马注册一个新公司，如今正是用人之际，大家都知道我原来专精在这个领域，我去巴拿马是不需要签证的，有我加入会更有利于公司业务在海外开展。就这样，我又回到了自己原来的行业。

在国外几年，基本不清楚国内的变化。其实2002—2008年，中国像开启了加速器，变化非常快。以薪资水平来讲，2002年我出国的时候，年薪只有5万元，

philosophy, history, and literature early in his life. In addition, I hope he would not, as I did, wait until reaching the age of fifty to start reflecting. "Progress in studies comes from diligence and is retarded by indolence; success comes from forethought, while thoughtlessness will lead to failure." No matter what age you are, you should be diligent in your thinking and sensitive in your actions, thinking about what kind of person you want to be in your life and what contributions you want to make to the society, instead of focusing on things such as enjoying a steak today and skiing tomorrow. These things are superficial; a true gentleman must cherish lofty aspirations instead of seeking a momentary pleasure.

V. The Zero-point Is Also a Starting Point

I received a phone call from one of my former colleagues, who told me that the group would soon set up a new company in Panama and there was an urgent need for qualified personnel. They knew that I had the expertise in this field and didn't need a visa to go to Panama. I could help boost the company's business in overseas markets if I would join it. This was how I came back to the industry I had been in.

Having been abroad for several years, I was not quite clear about the changes taking place in China. In fact, China underwent rapid changes during 2002-

而2007年，我这样的工程师在国内的年薪大概是35万~40万元，和我在巴拿马的薪资差不多，而且基本上很多家庭都有私家车了，国内发展之快是在国外的我们无法想象的。而且2007年开始，国家要求央企逐渐走出海外，这个关头很多集团都缺人，海外怎么做？谁来做？都是要面临的现实问题。在这个新形势下，我的专业和海外生活经验结合就比较稀缺。2008年，曾经的领导给我打电话让我回上海工作，条件由我来提。我说，不谈条件，您亲自打电话，我一定回来。

就这样，时隔七年，我和太太再次回到国内，儿子留在加拿大上大学。虽然回到了上海，但我负责的是海外业务拓展，基本活动范围还是在国外，前期主要负责的区域是拉丁美洲。随着业务不断拓展，我也常驻过巴西，在巴西过了50岁生日。当时我和公司签署的只是劳务合同，每三年续签一次，2021年刚好到了续签阶段，公司出了一些新政策，想派我入驻俄罗斯。但我太太希望我不要在外面漂，最好不要离开上海附近，就这样，我加入了施璐德。

2008. My annual salary was only 50,000 RMB yuan in 2002, the year when I went abroad; by 2007, however, the annual salary of an engineer like me in China had increased to 350,000-400,000 RMB yuan, similar to my salary in Panama. Moreover, many families in China began to have their own cars. All these changes were beyond our imagination. From 2007 on, central SOEs were required by the government to "go overseas," many of which were short of personnel. What should they do to "go overseas," and who would do it? These were the problems they must face. Then the combination of my expertise and overseas experience was relatively scarce. In 2008, the former leader called me and invited me to come back to Shanghai; I was free to list my requirements. "Nothing special." I said. "You've made the call, and I will come back for sure."

Thus, my wife and I returned to China after seven years, while my son stayed in Canada to attend university. Although I returned to Shanghai, I was responsible for overseas business development and for most of the time worked abroad, mainly in the region of Latin America in the early stages. With the expansion of business, I once stayed in Brazil for a long period of time, where I celebrated my fiftieth birthday. At that time, I only signed a labor contract with the company, which was renewed every three years, and in 2021 when it was time for renewal, the company came out with

6. 结缘施璐德，从相见恨晚到惺惺相惜

我和施璐德的缘分始于董事长池勇海先生。2016年初我们因为哥伦比亚的安基奥基亚港口项目结识，原本我们是沟通项目技术支持和合作的问题，这一聊却相见恨晚。谈话结束前，池总邀请我回上海后给施璐德员工做个讲座，专门说一说海外工程该怎么做。所以在我正式入职施璐德前，差不多每年都会来公司和员工们进行交流，或做专题讲座。

some new policies and wanted me to work in Russia. However, my wife wanted me to stop drifting and work in a place preferably not far away from Shanghai. Therefore, I joined CNOOD.

VI. Brought Together by Destiny

My relationship with CNOOD began with its chairman, Mr. Dennis Chi. We got to know each other at the beginning of 2016 because of the Antioquia port project in Colombia. We were supposed to discuss about technical support and cooperation for the project; when we began to talk, both of us regretted we hadn't meet sooner. Before the end of the conversation, Dennis invited me to give a lecture about overseas projects to people in his company when I was back in Shanghai. So I came to the company almost every year to communicate with

在分享过程中，我就感觉到施璐德的企业氛围和其他公司不同，从每一位同事充满求知欲的眼神中就能看得到。即使有些知识和他们没什么关系，他们也会非常认真地学，这种学习气氛和积极向上的力量体现在每一位员工身上。

2021年在考虑接下来的职业规划时，我想既然已经在央企干了大半辈子，是不是也要去体验一下民企的工作氛围。到我这个年纪，也不担心自己失业了，如果要按自己的心意来选择一种工作环境，施璐德一定是首选。

在职场多年，我体会到公司的企业文化大致分为两种：一种是说出来的企业文化，一种是干出来的企业文化。过去在央企和国企工作，我发现，它们的企业文化大多很难理解和落实，或者说平时就没有按照企业文化的标准去践行。一个不能走进员工大脑的企业文化基本形同虚设，变成了单纯的口号。而施璐德是一家既把企业文化时刻挂在嘴上，也能积极落实在行动中的企业。

people there, and sometimes I would give a special lecture to them.

During the process of sharing, I had a strong feeling that there was a different atmosphere at CNOOD, which could be seen from the inquisitive eyes of everyone working there. They would learn everything earnestly even if the knowledge was irrelevant to their jobs. This atmosphere of learning, together with the energy of optimism, was displayed by every member of the company.

In 2021, when I was considering my next career plan, I thought that since I had been working in SOEs for most of my life, maybe I should also experience the working atmosphere of private enterprises. At my age, I was no longer worried about losing my job, so if I could choose a working environment as I liked it, CNOOD would doubtlessly be my first choice.

After the many years in workplace, I have come to the conclusion that there are roughly two types of corporate cultures: the corporate culture as the result of *talking* and that as the result of *doing*. When I worked in SOEs, I found most of their corporate cultures hard to understand and hard to put into practice; they were not complied with in daily work from the very beginning. Any corporate culture that is not in people's mind exists in name only, nothing more than a slogan. CNOOD is a company that not only talks about its corporate culture but

《小王子》中有一句经典的话：如果你想造一艘船，不要抓一批人来搜集材料，不要指挥他们做这个做那个，你只要教他们如何渴望大海就够了。企业文化其实就是这样一个东西，首先它能够让大家都向往某一种境界，至于具体该做什么，这是第二步才去考虑的。

当然，我选择施璐德也是因为对池勇海先生的个人认同。池总是一个难得的身居高位却能放得下自己的人，作为开拓者，尽管他有时候很独断，但他一旦看准一个问题，或者被说服以后，他的执行程度比提问题的人还要坚决。施璐德一向是内举不避亲、外举不避怨的，所以有很多同学、朋友等都会一起加入公司，关系网略有复杂，但只要我发现项目上的问题跟他提出来，同时他也认同我的观点，那

also actively puts it into practice.

There is a famous sentence in the novel *The Little Prince* by Antoine de Saint-Exupéry, "If you want to build a ship, don't drum up people together to collect wood and don't assign them tasks and work, but rather teach them to long for the endless immensity of the sea." Corporate culture is exactly such a thing: first of all, it makes everyone long for a certain goal. And you will consider what they should do specifically only in the second step.

Of course, I chose CNOOD also because I personally identify with its chairman, Mr. Dennis Chi. Dennis is a rare person who humbles himself despite being in a high position. As a pioneer, he is sometimes arbitrary, but once he sees a problem or is convinced by someone, he is more determined than the person who reports the problem in overcoming it. CNOOD always adopts the policy

他立马就会告诉对方停掉，从来不会因为私人关系影响到工作。

最让我敬佩的就是池总的志向。他创办企业的初衷不是要成为富翁，要为自己赚多少钱，而是希望带着大家一起成长。施璐德的企业文化中有一条是"共创、共治、共享"，所有人都成长了，他就非常欣慰。

究竟该如何去成长，是需要进一步讨论思考的问题。就像"中国梦，我的梦"，大家都觉得这个梦很好，但怎么实现？梦想和实现之间是有断层的。施璐德近几年发展很快，企业智慧也在不断生发，但它就像一个少年在生长发育期，个子长得很快，但骨架来不及生长，容易缺钙。我们现在需要补钙，要让我们的系统更强，能够支撑住我们的理念；不能头脑在飞，身体还在原地跟不上节奏；在飞速成长的同时，也要考虑回过头来去夯实。

of "recommending people regardless of their relationship with yourself." Therefore, there are many classmates and friends working in the company, forming a slightly complex network. But as long as I find a problem with a project and he agrees with me, he will immediately tell them to stop it. He never allows himself to be influenced by personal relationships.

One thing for which I admire Dennis the most is his ambition. He started a business not to become a rich man or to make a lot of money for himself, but to bring others to grow together. The corporate culture of CNOOD is about being "created, managed, and shared by all". He will be gratified if all the members of the company have achieved growth.

It is a question to be further discussed that how should we achieve growth. Take the concept "Chinese dream, my dream" for instance. We all agree that it's a wonderful dream, but what should we do so that it'll come true? There is a gap between a dream and the reality. CNOOD has been growing really fast in recently years, with its wisdom growing at the same time. Nevertheless, it's like an adolescent who becomes taller every day while the bone growth is a little slower and will probably cause calcium deficiency. Now we need to take in more calcium, making our system strong enough to support our ideas. It won't do if you mind is flying in the sky while your body is stuck in the same place. When we

以上是我选择施璐德的原因。至于我能为施璐德带来什么，在入职前，我也认真思考过。施璐德是一个国际化公司，主营海外业务，而我差不多有将近二十年的时间，都在接触海外市场和海外文化，在这方面有比较深厚的基础。

7. 感知行业使命，俯首甘为孺子牛

"五十而知天命"，我确实是从50岁开始渐起内观意识，开始思考人生，思考自己的价值和对职业的贡献。如今到了60岁，与其列举贡献，倒不如提出一些工作中待解决的问题，结合我的经验帮助年轻人建立一个可升级的思维管道。

多年来，我最愿意做的就是和年轻人沟通。尤其是加入施璐德以后，很多年轻人都和我儿子同龄，我一直和他们保持高频率的互动，有意识地深入交流，大部分时间是把我的一些领悟、顿悟和他们分享。这样做的目的，无非是希望他们少走弯路，让他们不要等到我这个年龄才认识到一些问题的实质或本质。如果能经由我的经验缩短他们的生长期，降低试错成本，也是一件有益的事。虽说"早成者未必有成，晚达者未必不达"，花开花落各有周期，但向上求索、向下扎根是可持续的。如果有改良的土壤和环境的加持，即

are growing fast, we should get around and lay a solid foundation for our growth.

These are the reasons why I have chosen CNOOD. I also thought seriously about what I could bring to CNOOD, a multinational company focusing on overseas businesses. As a person with nearly twenty years' experience in overseas markets and cultures, I believe that I have a good background in this aspect.

VII. The Perception of My Mission in the Industry

Confucius said, "At fifty, I knew the decrees of Heaven." Actually, I started to have "inward observation" and think about my life, my values and my contributions to my career from the age of fifty. Now that I am sixty, instead of listing my contributions, I would like to raise some issues to be solved in my work and, drawing on my experience, help young people develop an upgradable tool of thinking.

Over the years, what I am most willing to do is to communicate with young people, especially after joining CNOOD. Many young people here are the same age as my son, and I have been interacting with them frequently. I consciously carry out in-depth communication with them, mostly sharing my understanding and insights. I do this because I hope they will make less detours so that they will not wait until my age to see the nature of certain problems. It will be beneficial if I can draw on my personal

使不快，也能更坚挺。

我曾经和公司的年轻人探讨过一个问题：有些项目好像很难，比如在欧洲某个国家竞标一个项目，对比之下觉得我们好多条件不具备，没法去做。这样的观念该如何破？

首先，学会对自己提问：别人叫我们报价，他看中我们的是什么？为什么是我们，不是另外一个公司？如果不思考这个问题，找不到答案，就相当于找不到目标，变成无的放矢。连对方的真实需求都不知道，那我们报出去的价格方案想让对方接受的概率就会很低。

其次，如果总是觉得这个项目没有我们，别人也能做，直接放弃掉，就会让机会白白溜走。我们最终的目的是要把握住机会，促进成长。所以更好的思考角度是：为什么不是我们？为什么对方没选我们？这样过滤出的就是我们的短板，考验的就是我们成事的态度了。有短板没问题，能不能克服？怎么克服？经常这样思

experience to make them grow faster with a smaller cost of trial and error. As an old saying goes, "Those who achieve fame and fortune early in life may not retain what they have for the rest of their lives, and those who get there late in life may not be any less successful." Flowers bloom and fall according to their own cycles, and yet it's always sustainable to explore upwards and take root downwards. When they are supported by improved soil and environment, they will grow more steadily, even if not very fast.

I once discussed a problem with the young people in the company: how can we get rid of the idea that we are not well prepared to bid for a seemingly difficult project, for instance a project in an European country?

First, learn to ask yourself the following questions: What does someone see in us when they inquire us for a quote? Why does the client choose us instead of other companies? If we don't think about these questions and can't find the answers, we just lose our target without knowing the real needs of our clients, and it is unlikely that the price we offer will be accepted.

Second, if we simply give up a project because we believe that it could be done without us, we'll miss opportunities for nothing. Our ultimate goal is to seize the opportunity and promote our growth. So there is a better way to think about it: Why not us? Why hadn't the client chosen us? By asking these questions,

考，机会才会更多。

思考角度变了，局面往往就会跟着变。所以每次开业务会，我都会为大家提供多个视角，以期产生更多共振。这个可能是我这些年做得更多的。

年轻的时候，我习惯用经手的数额、做成项目的利润来评定职场业绩，而近十年来我最常做的其实是帮助大家升维。公司每接到一个新工程、开拓一个新版图、打造一个新专业，带"新"的项目大多会先交给我，因为我会用一个更全局的思维方式和视角去组织投标，而不是凭经验。只凭经验很容易陷入瓶颈，依据项目本身的特点去做，才能因地制宜，提升可能性。

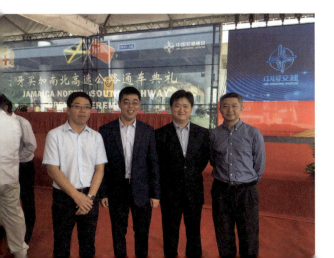

we'll be able to identify our weakness, and it is our attitude towards fulfilling things that will be tested. It's OK if we have weaknesses. Can we overcome them? What should we do to overcome them? Only by thinking in this way can we have more opportunities.

Once we begin to think from a different perspective, the overall picture will change with it. Every time we have a business meeting, I will provide multiple perspectives in the hope of producing more synergy. This is probably what I have done more often over the past few years.

When I was young, I was used to assessing people's performance by the amount of money they handled and the profit they made. What I have been doing most often in the past ten years, however, is to help people upgrade. Whenever the company gets a new project, opens up a new field, or creates a new profession, most of the "new" projects will be given to me, because I will prepare the bidding in a more holistic way of thinking, rather than rely on experience. We are likely to come across a bottleneck if we rely merely on our experience. We can adapt to local conditions and enhance the possibilities of success only if we work on projects according to their uniqueness.

就像戏剧导演赖声川先生提出的一个概念——"双视线"。放在做项目里，我们可以理解为一只眼睛盯着项目的特质，另一只眼睛看到整体。思考项目特质的时候，能意识到这个部分和整体的关系，这样思路容易变清晰。以前我们看问题容易从下面往上走，而我们现在看问题可能要从最根本的原则出发，然后再细化。

还有一个是考虑问题的思维方式。人的惯性利用好了可以提升效率，利用不好反而成为桎梏。很多人在做事时，总爱思考"我怎么去做"。一旦把"我"前置，就已经陷入片面视角。怎么调整呢？要学会把"事"前置，思考"这件事情应该怎么去做。"

商业的模式是达到利益、效益的最大化。以前讲究"唯我独尊"，以排挤和打压的方式做商业，但历史告诉我们这种思维模式难以长久，它可能会帮你在一个项目上赚得盆满钵满，但也止步于此。因为商业合作需要诚信和符合双方利益的平衡点，这也是现下想成功需要的一个前提条件。

施璐德之所以这些年发展得很快，和前几年努力取得很多国外总承包商的信任

Just like the concept of "dual vision" proposed by the theater director Stan Lai, we should have one eye focusing on the uniqueness of the project and the other eye seeing the whole picture. It is easier to get a clear idea if we are aware of the relationship between the part and the whole when we think of the uniqueness of a project. We used to approach a problem from the bottom up, but now we may have to start with the fundamental principle before we break the matters down.

There is another issue about the way of thinking when we approach a problem. Human inertia can be used to improve efficiency, but it'll become an obstacle if it isn't used in the right way. Many people like to think about "How should I do it?" when doing things. Once "I" is emphasized, they are already trapped by a one-sided view. Then how should they make a difference? They should learn to attach emphasis on "it" and think about "How should it be done?"

Business is all about maximizing the benefits and efficiency. We used to stick to the principle of "put-me-first" and did business by excluding and crowding out competition. But history has told us that this is an unsustainable way of thinking, which may help you make a pile on a project and then stop there. Business cooperation requires honesty as well as a balance in line with the interests of both sides, which is a prerequisite for success.

The rapid development of CNOOD during the past few years is inseparable

分不开，所以一些项目后来都不招标了，直接谈价钱。盘点以往工作中做得好、做得顺畅的项目，基本都有这样的成功路径，合作的首要前提是和对方达成共识，让对方看到你的诚信，列出的合同条件公平，该挣的钱要挣，不该挣的钱不要惦记，这样很多事情就很容易做了，大家矛盾也会变小，把精力都放在思考如何成事上。利益，要平衡，不要压制，总想搞什么障眼法，那我们如何累积口碑？池总在他的《共同利益论》中提到："全人类共同利益是人类赖以维系生存与发展的主要前提和基本条件。"这是普遍规律。

如今的中国正从"高速增长"进入"高质量发展"的阶段，施璐德也正处于这样的阶段。所以，跳出窠臼重新建立我们的价值观，重新理解格局，已经迫在眉睫。正如叶剑英元帅所说，"宏观在宇，微观在握"，面对复杂纷呈的问题，关键要做到大处着眼，小处着手。

from the efforts made in the previous years to gain the trust of general contractors in overseas markets. As a result, for some of the later projects, we just negotiated on the price directly, without a call for bidding. When we review the successful projects, we can always find such a path. The primary prerequisite for cooperation is a consensus with each other, so that your integrity could be seen by the other party. Terms in a contract should always be fair; you earn the money you are supposed to earn, and forget the money you ought not earn. In this way, many things will become easy, and we will have fewer conflicts, focusing on making things happen. Interests are to be balanced, not to be suppressed. How could we build up a reputation if we always resort to disguising tricks? Dennis wrote in his book *Common Interest Theory*, "The common interests of all mankind are the major prerequisites and basic conditions for mankind's survival and development." This is a universal law.

China is now moving from the stage of "high-speed growth" to that of "high-quality development," and so is CNOOD. Therefore, it is urgent to break out of the rut to re-establish our values and re-understand the big picture. Just as Marshal Ye Jianying said, "With the macro in the infinite space, we hold the micro in our hands." Facing a tangled skein of problems, it's crucial to think big and act small.

8. 凡是过往皆为序章

60年一路走来，个中滋味能讲出来的，不过十之一二，很多感受不足为外人道。

儿时，父母并没有对我们的三观进行系统性建设，没有告诉我们该读什么书、该做什么思考，只是身体力行地让我们领会到该如何为人、如何处事，虽无言，但对精神的塑造影响深远。

后来一路求学，对学习没有太认真，只是凭借一点点自诩的聪明和机灵过关斩将考入大学。1979年的大学生真的是"天之骄子"，提到"大学生"都说了不起，"物以稀为贵"在那个年代是能充分感受到的。在我们的意识里，"大学生"就是世界的尽头，年纪轻轻就达到顶峰，剩下的几十年玩就得了。

后来到了加拿大，很多人来跟我讲，基督教会会帮助你。我对新鲜事物一向不会拒绝，所以也尝试了去教堂听牧师传道。但我自小受无神论影响颇深，只能听到教堂里的回音，却感觉不到与神对话，入教会一事不了了之。

VIII. What's Past Is Prologue

Along my journey of sixty years, I can tell but a small portion of what I have tasted, while most the feelings are not worth mentioning to others.

When I was a child, my parents did not do much to shape our values, nor did they tell us what to read and what to think about. They let us understand, by their own practice, how we should behave or deal with things. Though wordless, they have exerted a profound impact on shaping of our mind.

Later in my education, I was not very serious about it and managed to pass the college entrance examination just by a little bit of self-proclaimed intelligence and resourcefulness. In 1979, college students were really the "favored sons of the Heaven," who were highly thought of by all — a perfect demonstration of the saying "Rare things are precious." We believed that being a college student was the zenith of the world, a peak at a young age, and we had nothing else to do for the next decades but enjoy ourselves.

When I arrived in Canada, many people told me that the Christian church would help me. I never refused new things, and I tried to go to church and listen to the sermons. However, I was deeply influenced by atheism since childhood; I could only hear the echoes inside the cathedral, failing to have dialogues with God. In the end, I did not join the church.

50岁那年,我参加了中学同学组织的聚会,大家商量着毕业30年了,是否要出一本书,把我们这么多年的经历总结一下。组织出书的同学是一位大学教授,她觉得我的经历要比别人多一点,希望我能贡献一篇文章。直到这时,我才意识到自己已经50岁了,仔细思量,发现我一直没什么明确的目标,风往哪吹我就往哪跑,更未想过安静地坐下来思考人生意义、人生价值和对社会的贡献,只是顺时顺势地生活了50年,那接下来的人生该怎么过呢?

2021年看了一本书叫《百岁人生》,一位英国作家写的。看过后我对人生有了新的理解,也更了解自己在潜意识中对生命是如何感知的。我们无法预测生物学上的寿命,像我的父母,如今年至耄耋依旧健康地生活着,如果我也能活到这个年龄,那后面的三四十年,难道一直是退休状态吗?答案肯定是不,我还有很多事情想做没去做,还有很多体验未完成。从年龄上来讲,60岁可能要考虑退休了,但"退休"这个词对我来说只是一个概念。想想老干部活动室和广场舞,好像离我还很远,毕竟前几天我刚在足球场上和一群年轻球友比拼了两个多小时,虽然我是球场上年龄最大的。

At the age of fifty, I attended a party of my high-school classmates. Then we talked about publishing a book thirty years after graduation to sum up our experiences over the past years. The classmate who managed the publication affairs was a university professor, and she hoped that I could contribute an article for she believed that I had a richer experience than others. It was only then that I realized I was already fifty years old, and when I thought about it, I discovered that I had never had a clear goal in my life and that I had always run wherever the wind blew. It never occurred to me to sit down quietly and ponder over the meaning and value of my life and the contributions I made to the society. What I had done was to follow the trend in the fifty years. What kind of life would I live in the future?

In 2021 I read a book by a British writer, *The 100-Year Life: Living and Working in an Age of Longevity*. After reading it, I have a new understanding of life and how I perceive it in my subconscious. We can't predict the biological life expectancy; my parents, for instance, are still living in good health now over the age of eighty. If I should be able to live to that age, will I stay in retirement for the next thirty or forties years? The answer is definitely no. There are still many things I want to do and many experiences I have yet to accomplish. In terms of age, I may have to consider retirement at the age of sixty, but

人生很多时候急不得，需要一个契机让我们顿悟。

如果 60 岁是一个全新的起点，我想接下来我会和自己的人生进行一次"明心见性"的对话。

the word "retirement" is no more than a concept to me. Both entertainment center for senior citizens and public square dancing seemed far away to me; after all, I just played soccer with a group of young men for more than two hours a few days ago, despite being the oldest on the field.

For most of the time, we are not supposed to rush in our lives, but need an opportune moment for a sudden enlightenment.

If the age of sixty is a completely new starting point, I think I will have a dialogue with my own life to "see the nature by enlightened mind."

首先，从阅读中领悟。过去的人都信奉一句话，"学好数理化，走遍天下都不怕"，那个年代认为学习不好的人才去学文科。现在，随着年龄增长，阅历丰富，才慢慢感觉到文学家、哲学家的伟大，孕育思想是很艰辛的过程。

近几年我开始体会到阅读的重要性，也借由阅读来拓展思想边界。最近这段时间开始关注中国的儒释道文化，每天开车上下班途中听十三经注释，了解"道"是怎么回事，人们为什么愿意献身宗教。虽然我没有那种境界，但不妨碍我去探索。

人在有一些阅历和体验之后，再开卷能够更多领会到书中理论背后的含义。比如佛教里面经常提到的"缘起性空"这几个字究竟什么意思，年轻时的我很难理解，但岁月和经验却能辅助我逐渐体悟。我认为这是一种递进式理解。

First, I will form an understanding by reading books. People used to believe that "whoever has a good command of math and sciences will have no fear for his future career." In those years, we thought that liberal arts were only for those students with poor academic performance. Now, with an older age and richer experiences, I have gradually come to understand the greatness of writers and philosophers, as well as the hardships in giving birth to new ideas.

In recent years, I have begun to realize the importance of reading and tried to expand my mental boundaries through reading. I have started to pay attention to Confucianism, Buddhism and Taoism in Chinese cultural tradition. I listen to the annotated version of the "Thirteen Classics of Confucianism" when driving on my way to and from work every day, in an attempt to understand what the Tao is all about and why people are willing to devote themselves to religion. Though without that kind of spirit, I don't find any obstacle that will stop me from exploring.

People can understand better the meaning of the theories in books when they have seen the world. For example, the words "dependent-arising and emptiness" often mentioned in Buddhist texts were incomprehensible to me when I was a young man; however, age and experience have really helped me to gain insights on its true meaning. I think this is a kind of progressive understanding.

我刚工作时，被分配在教育科当了两年老师，虽然专业并不对口，但大学生是稀缺资源，各部门不管对不对口，先抢到人再说。

在教育科是要给单位职工上课的，给谁讲呢？比我大七八岁的老职工。那一批人没机会学好课程，要在单位进行文化补习，加强素质升级，我就负责为他们讲初中物理，前一天晚上先备课，第二天就上课。在备课的过程中发现，上学那会儿我只是记住了概念，并不明白原理，现在要给学生讲这些概念，就需要去挖掘源头，借由这次机会我才搞明白牛顿定律究竟是怎么回事。后来这一批职工参加上海市统考，拿到卷子后我一看考题，觉得太简单了，但我的学生考完出来都说难。

这说明学生视角和老师视角完全不同，我们大多时候只能立足当下去理解所见所学，势必会有局限性，但把知识放在时间线上或另一个维度上再看，就豁然开朗了。

I worked in the education department as a tutor for two years after I started my career. The work didn't match my academic training, for all the departments were vying for college graduates who were scarce in those days.

As a member of the education department, it was my job to give lectures to the employees in our company, who were seven or eight years older than me. Without the opportunity to do well in school subjects, they must take a remedial course to make up for their weaknesses in education background. I was responsible for teaching them physics of junior-high-school level. When I was preparing my lesson the night before the class, I found that I had only memorized the concepts in school, but did not understand the underlying principles. I had to start from the beginning if I was going to give a clear explanation of these concepts to my students. It was by this chance that I finally figured out what Newton's laws are really about. Later, when they entered for the unified examination in Shanghai, I took a look at the test paper and thought it was too easy. However, my students all agreed that it was very difficult.

This is an example of the huge difference between learning from a student's perspective and that from a teacher's perspective. Most of the time, we can only understand what we see and what we learn from the present perspective, which is bound to have limitations; however, when we look at the

其次，继续在生活中修心修行。外界对于工程师或多或少会有刻板印象，但工程师只是职业，工作之余我也有一些兴趣爱好。

我喜欢运动，不是跑步也不是游泳，而是带有对抗性的运动，这样我会更忘我地参与其中。

我喜欢做饭，曾经跟老父亲学了几道正宗的淮扬菜，后来无论走到什么地方，我都有关注当地特色菜肴的习惯，现在可以做一桌混搭的中西餐。年轻时我常说，宁做十道菜，不刷一个碗。所以从单身汉聚会到家庭、亲友团聚，站在锅台边上的一定是我。当然年轻时的豪言只是豪言而已，现在我也会主动刷碗了。

我喜欢摄影，大学的时候买不起照相机，就把为数不多的零用钱花在了订《摄影世界》杂志上。1995年在缅甸工作时，有了点小积蓄，花了一千美元买了自己的第一台尼康单反，后来生活条件逐渐提升，就在家里配了一套洗影和放大机，全流程体验摄影的乐趣。

knowledge by the timeline or in another dimension, we will feel fully enlightened.

Second, I should continue to refine my heart and my practice in my daily life. There have been, more or less, stereotypes about engineers. For me, it's just a job, and I have some hobbies in my spare time.

I love sports, but not jogging or swimming. It has to be a game with confrontation so that I will be more devoted when playing it.

I love cooking, and have learned the recipes of a few authentic Huaiyang-style dishes from my father. Wherever I went, I would pay attention to the local cuisine. Now I can make a decent meal, mixing both Chinese and western foods. When I was younger, I would often say that I would rather cook ten dishes than wash a bowl. So from bachelor parties to family reunions, I was always the one standing at the kitchen range. Of course, the heroic remarks when I was young were no more than heroic words; now I will also volunteer to wash the bowls.

I love photography. When I couldn't afford a camera at college, I spent my pocket money on a subscription to the magazine *Photo World*. In 1995, when I was working in Myanmar I had some savings and spent 1,000 US dollars on my first Nikon SLR. Later with improved living conditions, I bought myself a photo processor and enlarger, so that I could experience the pleasure of photography through the whole process.

我喜欢自己动手做事，在加拿大时，我们一家三口一起在后院盖了一个15平方米的仓库，回到上海后，我也在自己的院子里做了一个花台式种菜园。

我也喜欢音乐，还加入了一个老同事的音乐发烧友群，自己组拼了一套性价比很高的 HiFi 系统。

再次，将自己历经岁月沉淀下来的经验逐渐转化为思想，见微知著。我一般很少会厌烦去做什么事情，相似的事情重复做，或者是完全没接触过的事情，我都能欣然接受。吸引我的不是事情本身，而是想通过做事来看看用我的知识、经验能不能触达到底层逻辑或更高维度。

以做海外项目为例，到国外做项目的人会经历两个认知阶段。第一阶段会带着对自己专业的足够自信，看到外国同行骄傲地说，我在工程领域已经从业多年，非常有经验。结果开会时发现对方一开口，都是从原理上深入浅出地剖析，我们忽然发现自己在专业方面就是个空架子，仅仅是有经验，而国内经验到了国外有极大可能会遭遇水土不服，这样很容易从骄傲一下子跌到自卑，觉得我们什么也不如人家。这时就要懂得跳出来看，在这个阶段，我们不了解他们，同样，他们也并不了解我们。到了第二阶段，如果还能够更进一步合作，大家就会更客观地了解彼此的优势和短板，这样双方就有了合作基

I like to do things by myself. When I was in Canada, the three members of my family built a fifteen-square-meter warehouse in our backyard, and when I returned to Shanghai, I made a flowerbed-style vegetable garden in our yard.

I also love music and joined a WeChat group of audiophiles with my former colleagues. I assembled a cost-effective HiFi system all by myself.

Third, I will gradually transform my experience that has survived the years into ideas, by which I'm able to see what's coming from small clues. I rarely get tired of doing something and would accept gladly doing similar things repeatedly or doing entirely new things. What attracts me is not the thing itself, but the desire to see if I can reach the underlying logic or a higher dimension with my knowledge and experience by doing it.

Take doing overseas projects as an example. People who go abroad to work on overseas projects will go through two cognitive stages. In the first stage, we will be full of confidence in our expertise and will say proudly to our foreign counterparts, "I've been in this field for many years, and I'm very experienced." But when our foreign counterparts begin to speak at the meeting, explaining complex ideas through underlying principles in plain terms, we would suddenly discover that we are nothing more than an empty shelf as regards our expertise. We have nothing but practical

础，逐渐产生共振，互相取长补短，真正达到效益最大化。而这两个阶段的过渡需要时间。

这些经验之谈，我希望接下来能够在和同行、年轻人交流的同时逐步变成更深层的思想，助力年轻人成长。

最后，体察物性之不同，统观行业之万象。回顾职业历程，从早期做技术人员到担任总工，从巴拿马再回到上海，我的工作都更偏向于技术。但也有前后期差异，前期我更多在做的是技术方案或策划，到海外以后发现，方案并不是最重要的，后期开始关注国内、国外同行业中不同公司在管理方面的差异。中国公司现在经验充足，实力很强，工程技术人员一大堆，最缺的就是管理人才。所以近十年间，我把更多的精力放在管理模式的思考上，阅读了彼得·德鲁克等管理大师的著述。

experience, which is very likely to be incompatible with the conditions in overseas markets. Therefore, it is very easy for us to fall from pride to inferiority, thinking that we are not as good as our foreign counterparts in all aspects. This is the moment when we must know how to look from outside, being aware of the fact that, in this stage, we and our foreign counterparts do not have a thorough understanding of each other yet. In the second stage, if there is still a chance for further cooperation, we will understand each other's strengths and weaknesses more objectively and create a basis for cooperation and synergy, achieving the maximization of economic efficiency. And it takes time to move from the first stage to the second one.

I hope that, when I communicate with my colleagues and young people, these experiences can be turned into deeper-level ideas and help young people achieve growth.

Lastly, I should perceive the difference in the nature of things, with a comprehensive view of the industry. Looking back on my career, my work is mainly technical, from being a technician in early days to being the chief engineer, from Panama and then back to Shanghai. But there was a difference: in earlier stages, I focused more on technical solutions or planning; after I went overseas, I discovered that solutions were not the most important and started to pay more attention to the differences in

我们同国外最大的差异就是思维。改革开放以来，国家一直鼓励我们走出去，多学习、多思考、多创新，但我们自小接受的是模式化的教育，给考试范围，有统一的标准答案，成年后想要突破着实不太容易。而国外的人思维是纲领性的，从根本原理上去思考问题，所以很多时候他们解决问题的能力就比我们要强很多。

管理，不仅仅是人力资源意义上的管理，身为管理者要更多思考如何从根本原理上去解决问题，这样对成长中的年轻人会更有帮助。

前一段时间，我和几位高中同学聚会，其中一位同学对我说：你从央企辞职去国外，走了一圈又回到国内，这不是又

management of different companies in the same industry in China and abroad. Chinese companies are now rich in experience and expertise, well-staffed with engineers and technicians; what they need most is management personnel. Therefore, I have spent more time in the past ten years on the management paradigms and have read the works by Peter Drucker and other management gurus.

In fact, the biggest difference between Chinese people and Westerners lies in the way of thinking. Since the adoption of the policy of reform and opening up, we have always been encouraged to "go out" to learn more, think more, and achieve more innovation. However, it is not that easy for us, who received "standardized" education in schools and colleges with standard tests and standard answers, to rid ourselves of old ideas. The Western way of thinking, on the other hand, is more programmatic, approaching a problem from the rationale behind it. Therefore, they are often more capable than us in solving problems.

Management is more than the management of human resources. Managers must think about the way to tackle problems by seeking the rationale behind them. By so doing, they can contribute more to the growth of young people.

The other day, I joined a small get-together with some of my high-school classmates. "You quit your job

回到原点了吗？这样你拿外国籍有什么意义呢？

可以说，正是因为走了这一大圈，我才明白站在平面看原点和站在立体空间看原点的视角是完全不同的。从平面看，我的回归就是倒退；而从立体空间看，是人生的进程，再次回归，这个原点和过去并不相同。正是有了这一段经历，我才有机会见天地、见众生，如今再见自己。我的眼界和思想早已不同，遇到事情也会更容易接纳、释然。

借用冯唐先生在《欢喜》中写到的一句话："初行路，读书，做人，潭很小，很静，太阳老是一掬笑容，山是山，水是水，我是我。"作为刚刚迈入60岁的新人，未来一路，还望与诸君同行共铸。

in a central SOE and went abroad, and now you have come back." One of them asked me, "Haven't you just returned to the origin after so big a circle? Then what's the point of acquiring a foreign citizenship?"

It is this big circle, I believe, that makes me aware of the fact that we have totally different perspectives when we look at the origin from somewhere in a plane or the three-dimensional space. Looking from somewhere in a plane, my returning is a retrogression; looking from somewhere in the three-dimensional space, however, it is part of the process of life, with the ending point different from the origin. It is because of this experience that I have had the opportunity to see the universe, the mortal beings, and finally, myself. My mental horizons, as well as my thought, has been different since very long ago, and it is easier to accept and understand things when I encounter them.

I would like to quote a sentence from Mr. Feng Tang's *Happiness*, "When I set out on the journey of life and began traveling and reading, the pond was very small and without ripple, and the sun was always smiling; I saw the mountains and waters as they were, and me as I was." As a person who has just reached the age of sixty, I hope to walk with you all in the journey ahead of us and cast brilliance together.

张 林
Lin Zhang

土木工程师，1983年毕业于华东水利学院（现河海大学）港口与工程专业。1983—2002年于中国交建第三航务工程局五公司工作，先后任教员、工段长、工程队长、项目经理、总工程师、副总经理等职。2002年移民加拿大，2006—2008年，中国港湾巴拿马分公司工作，任副总经理，负责市场开发和技术管理。2008—2021年中国交建第三航务工程局海外事业部副总经理兼主任工程师，负责美洲和俄罗斯的市场开发及海外工程技术管理。2021—2023年，施璐德亚洲有限公司总工程师，负责项目和技术管理。

Lin Zhang is a civil engineer who graduated from East China Institute of Water Resources (now Hohai University) majoring in port and waterway engineering. During 1983-2002, he worked in the No. Five Construction Company of CCCC Third Harbor Engineering Company as tutor, section chief, construction team leader, project manager, the chief engineer, and the deputy general manager. He emigrated to Canada in 2002, and worked at the Panama subsidiary of China Harbour Engineering Company (CHEC) as the deputy general manager for market development and technical management. He was the deputy general manager and staff engineer of the Overseas Business Department of CCCC Third Harbor Engineering Company during 2008-2021, responsible for market development and overseas project technical management in America and Russia. He has been the chief engineer of CNOOD ASIA LIMITED since 2021, focusing on project and technical management.

接纳普通，有度的人生更自在

Accepting Ordinariness, a Moderate Life Is More Comfortable

■ Andy Wei

写这篇文章时，回眸细数，2023年是我加入CNOOD的第十一个年头。其间，我完成了就业、深造、安家、结婚生女等人生大事。最初没有想法、没有主见、不自信的小伙子，在工作中不断历练，提高了能力，如今能在工作上独当一面，决策果断，充满自信；在生活中家庭和顺，太太贤惠，女儿可爱。

如果是拍电影，镜头里这时候应该会有窗明几净的办公室或会议室，一个衣衫笔挺、态度严谨的我穿行其中。

不知道如果这个故事真的拍成电影，观众的感受会怎样，如果我是观众，电影结束时我心里只会想：今天要按时下班回家，带女儿出去遛弯儿了。

As I write this article, I look back on my life and count: 2023 is my eleventh year in CNOOD, during which I have accomplished major life events, such as finding a job, postgraduate studying, settling down, getting married, and having a daughter. Originally an indecisive and unconfident young man with few opinions of his own, I have now enhanced my abilities through the constant trials at work. Now, at work, I can shoulder my responsibilities alone and take the lead, decisive and confident, and at home, I enjoy harmonious family life, with a virtuous wife and a cute daughter.

If my life was made into a movie, now, it would show a neat and tidy office or conference room, with me pacing in it, well-dressed and sternly mannered.

I don't know how the audience would feel if they really watched a film like this, but if I were among them, when the film ended, my only thought would be that I

对人的一生来说，十年算是一个里程碑，每一个用力生活的人，站在十年的时间节点上回看过去，都不免一番唏嘘。如果让我用一句话来概括自己在 CNOOD 的十年生活，我会说：这就是一个普通人普普通通的成长经历罢了。一个最普通的农村孩子，在大学刚毕业人生迷茫、看不到前景之时，做了一个普通的选择，加入了一个那时看起来还很普通的公司，自此十年间与公司同生共息、共同成长。

1. 英雄一闪而过，普通才是人生

有些人对"普通"这个词避而不谈，对破圈层、突破人生心存渴望，他们或多或少都有英雄梦，也偶尔会在深夜反反复复地畅想未来。我曾经也有过作家梦，想离职去读研、写作，认为写作才是理想的生活状态。如今经历时间洗礼，发现这不过是成长过程中的一段经历，对我来说，英雄是一闪而过的概念，普通才是真切的人生。

有一部电影叫《土拨鼠之日》，故事

should go home on time and take my girl out for a walk.

For a person's life, one decade is a milestone. When looking back on the past ten years, anyone who has lived an earnest life will undoubtedly be touched by deep and mixed emotions. If I should use one sentence to conclude my past decade at CNOOD, I would say that this was just an ordinary growth story of an ordinary person. A kid born into a most ordinary rural family made an ordinary choice when at a loss as to his future after graduation from college, joined a then ordinary-looking company, and then shared his destiny and grew together with the company for the next ten years.

I. Heroism Flashes by, While Ordinariness Lasts for Life

Some people detest the word "ordinary," and hold the aspiration to break the social stratum and move up the social ladder. They have more or less once dreamed about becoming a hero and might occasionally imagine the future again and again in deep nights. I once dreamed about becoming a writer and wanted to quit my job to go to graduate school and write, believing that only a life of writing constituted an ideal life. But now, as time has passed by, I find that dream to be only a phase of growing up. For me, heroism is just a concept that flashes by, while ordinariness is the true life.

There is a movie *Groundhog Day*,

情节其实并不复杂，讲的是在美国传统的土拨鼠日这一天，男主人公菲尔去小镇报道土拨鼠日庆典的新闻，一切都和前几年没什么不同，同样的流程，同样的播报词，同样的平淡无奇。在报道的第二天却发生了非常神奇的事情，每当他早晨醒来，都会回到相同的一天：永远都是2月2日，土拨鼠日。当天所发生的事情，就像是录像带一样反复播放，重复出现相同的人，每天起床都有同样的电台广播，同一个人会和他搭讪，餐厅老太太会重复和他聊天询问早餐和天气，路上会遇见同一位乞丐和卖保险的旧朋友，报道节目等，菲尔就此陷入了鬼打墙一样的循环中。

whose story is not complicated: on the traditional American holiday, Groundhog Day, the hero Phil went to a small town to report on the holiday celebrations. Everything was no different from the last year, with the same procedure, the same broadcast script, and the same ordinariness. But on the next day, something extraordinary happened. When Phil woke up in the morning, it would always repeat the same day—February 2, Groundhog Day! Everything that happened on that day would repeat themselves, like a video tape played over and over again: the same people would appear; the same radio broadcast was aired in the morning; the same person would engage in small talk with him; the same old lady at the restaurant would ask him about breakfast and weather; he would meet on his way the same beggar and the same insurance-selling friend; he would broadcast the same news report …. He was trapped in this endless daunting loop.

《土拨鼠之日》这部影片剧情简单，却受很多人喜爱，正是因为主人公菲尔所经历的日复一日，和大多数人的现实生活没什么不同，每天工作、生活，行动半径只有几千米，如此循环往复。影片带领观众进入情境，用窥视和伴随解答心中的那个问题：如何在相似的生活中寻求解脱？

我们的生活就像未杀青的影片，每天一帧一帧地过。影片之所以看起来有趣吸睛，都是剪辑师对普通元素的巧妙布局。试着把你认为枯燥无味的相似生活重新排列组合，普通就能变得真切且有趣。

2. 接纳现实，向下向内扎根

可能是自小的成长经历，让我练就了一项能力，就是充分认识到自己只是一个普通人，要学会接受现实。

大多数人在人生每一阶段的转折点，会面临"选择"，比如选择什么学校，选择什么公司，选择哪种生活方式。而在我的成长过程中，并没有那么多选择，甚至是没有其他选择，面前摆着的无论好坏对我来说就是最优解。这就像打牌，你盲抓了一副牌，牌局未尽，没机会重洗换牌，

The story of *Groundhog Day* is simple, but the movie is beloved by many people, because the daily routines that Phil went over again and again were no different from most people's real life. Every day, our work, life, and actions take place only within a radius of several kilometers, repeating themselves just like in a loop. The movie leads audience into such a scenario to take a glimpse at and try to answer the question buried in our mind: how to find relief in such self-repeating daily lives?

Our lives are like unfinished movies, passing frame by frame every day. Movies become interesting and eye-catching only after editors rearrange the seemingly ordinary elements. Try rearranging and reorganizing the similar life components that you consider boring and banal, and then ordinariness would become lovely and interesting.

II. Accept Reality, Be Pragmatic, and Explore Inward

Perhaps due to my upbringing, I have developed a special ability, which is to fully realize that I am just an ordinary person and that I need to learn to accept this reality.

At the turning point of each stage of life, most people will face choices, such as choosing a school, choosing a company, and choosing a lifestyle. But as I grew up, I did not have so many options, sometimes no other option at all. No matter good or bad, whatever available before me was

唯一能做的就是把手上这副牌打好。这就锻炼我在面对事情时，更多思考的是如何将现有的资源价值最大化，而不是把精力放在期望、期待上。

很多人在拿到烂牌时第一反应是沮丧、抱怨，心里期待着下一次我要换个位置，手气好一些，抓到一副好牌一定翻身。现实是，人生总是喜忧参半的，无论你选到什么牌，我们能把握的也只有当下这一部分。

十年过去，随着职场升迁、家庭组建，我能选择的机会明显变多了，但在工作和生活中，我大部分的选择依旧是：都行。

前几年曾有过赴缅工作的经历。当时接到赴缅电话时，我正陪太太在医院做孕前体检，既然公司有需要，我没犹豫就答应了。项目计划是三个月，在CNOOD，三个月的差旅完全正常，既然领导选择我，我不一定是最优秀的，却肯定是当下最合适的。后来，这个项目实际运作了近一年，一是因为项目本身的复杂程度，二是突发疫情导致购票回国也着实不易。面对严峻形势，我也经历了多次内耗和调整。你会发现，生活有时会给你选择，但

the best chance I had. It was like playing cards: you draw your cards blindly and cannot switch cards until the end of the game, so the only thing you can do is to play well with the cards you have. This has trained me to focus on maximizing the value of existing resources when faced with difficulties, rather than making wishes or dwelling on expectations.

A lot of people immediately get frustrated and complain about it when they are dealt a bad hand when playing cards, wishing for better seats or better luck to bring them better cards next time. But in reality, life is always filled with both happiness and sorrow. No matter which cards you have drawn, they are the only resources that you can leverage at the moment.

Ten years have passed. With promotion at work and the formation of a family, I clearly feel that there are more opportunities for me to choose from now. However, whether at work or in my personal life, my attitude most of the time is still "anything will do."

Several years ago, I went to Myanmar on a business trip. When I got the phone call about that assignment, I was at the hospital, accompanying my wife for pre-pregnancy check-up. Since the company was in need, I accepted the assignment without much hesitation. The project was scheduled to last three months, which was completely normal for us at CNOOD. Since my superiors chose me, I must have been the most appropriate

你无论怎么组合都不会达到最完美的状态，立足当下，用好手上现有的资源，做好自己能做的，才是根本。

同事对我的友好评价是：Andy 蛮谦虚的，没有架子，愿意做事情，不推脱，有担当。其实，这只是我的做事习惯，遇到情况先思考现在手上有多少资源，这些资源该怎么用才能把事情做好、完成，而不是先去权衡事情的大小和利弊。权衡太多会陷入得失计较，也会忽略认知自我、打造专业实力、向下扎根的契机。

就像《土拨鼠之日》中的主人公菲尔，在一次次想逃避日复一日的生活却无果时，开始对生活失去信心，并一度消极，没想到更恐怖的是，他也无法杀死自己，无论他如何自杀，第二天一早，都会好好的躺在床上等待着早晨的到来。

one for the task at that moment, despite not necessarily being the best. In the end, I stayed in Myanmar for almost a year to implement the project, partly because the project was quite complicated and partly because it was rather difficult to fly back home due to the sudden pandemic. Faced with such a grave situation, I also went through several cycles of self-attrition and self-adjustment. You will sometimes find that even though life offers you choices, you still cannot reach the optimal state, no matter how you choose. The only thing you can do is to ground yourself, use what you have, and do what you can—this is the basis for everything.

My colleagues once praised me as a quite humble and unpretentious person who is willing to take on difficult tasks and shoulder responsibilities. In fact, this is just my habit in dealing with tasks, which is to directly evaluate what resources I have and how to use them to reach the optimal result, rather than weigh up the pros and cons of taking up the task first. Dwelling too much on the costs and benefits will trap you there and make you miss the opportunities to understand yourself, enhance professional capability, and be more pragmatic.

Take Phil, the hero in *Groundhog Day*, as an example. With his repeated failed attempts to escape the loop, Phil began to lose confidence in life and became pessimistic. But he became even more horrified when he found out that he could not even kill himself. No matter

在经历了许多并置之死地以后，菲尔终于大彻大悟，既然无法逃避这一切，不如过好这么一天吧。于是他开始改善自己的人际关系，去努力学习一切，而不单纯是为了什么目的，尽情享受生活。最后，在经历了无数的2月2日后，他发现他的生活已完全不一样，一年才去一次的小镇上他认识了所有的人，并且和他们都发生了各种故事，变成一个广受欢迎的好人。

电影最后，改变后的菲尔终于在一天之内打动了女主角丽塔的心，并且共度良宵。而在第二天起床以后，菲尔发现丽塔并没有消失，而是还在他身边，时间也变成了2月3日。那无休止的土拨鼠日总算过去了。

当你觉得人生受困，其实更多是内心的自我束缚，生活是一面镜子，目之所及的一切都是你心之所想。生活会因我的变化而变化，但我不会因为生活的变化而变化。稳住初心，向下向内扎根，充分抓住自己的确定性，以更从容的状态做好事，做成事，当然，无论是大事还是小事。

how he committed suicide, the next morning, he would still wake up in his own bed, waiting for the beginning of yet another same day.

After numerous failed suicide attempts, Phil finally reached epiphany: now that the loop seemed inescapable, why not try to live the day well? Phil began to improve his relations with others and try to learn everything, not to achieve a specific goal, but simply to enjoy life. In the end, after living countless loops of February 2, he found his life completely different. Before, he only visited the small town once a year, but now, he knew all the residents there and had personal stories with every one of them, making him a very popular guy with a decent reputation.

At the end of the movie, having undergone all these changes, Phil managed to win the heart of Rita, the heroine, within one day and spent the night with her. The next day, Phil woke up to find that Rita did not disappear and was still beside him. It was February 3! The loop finally ended.

When you feel trapped, it actually reflects more of the self-restraints in your mind than real constraints in life. Life is like a mirror, and what you see reflects what you think. Life changes along with me, but I do not change along with life. Hold on to your initial aspirations, be pragmatic, and explore inward to fully take hold of your own certainties. This way, you will be able to remain calm and

3. 集中优势兵力出击

也许是因为自小到大从来选择不多，所以就养成了抓核心、抓要点办成事的习惯。正如《孙子兵法·虚实篇》进攻体系里所讲的一条，要集中优势兵力出击，而想要用兵如水、随形而变，则先要夯实战略思想，充分掌握战术原则。我的工作原则之一，就是无论遇到什么，都先了解底层逻辑和结构，这样才能以不变应万变。也许就是这样，才有了如今大家眼中的我：能处理好大多数事情。

这项看起来厉害的技能，也不过是在重复又重复 / 普通又普通的事情中练就的。如果说难得，我想难得的是愿意在十数年中下日日之功吧。

每个人对事的理解不同，所以遇事的反应也会不同，进入公司十年后，我的工作和生活环境发生了很大改变，不变的是我依旧还是普通人过着普通的生活。就像穿衣服这件小事，过去条件没那么好，我对着装并没多大的要求，能穿、干净、舒适就行；现在我依旧没啥要求，能穿、干

relaxed and deliver the best results for all kinds of tasks.

III. Gather All Strong Forces to Launch an Attack

Perhaps because I did not get to choose much when I grew up, I formed the habit of accomplishing tasks through grasping the key points and core requirements. In *The Art of War*, Sun Tzu discussed how to launch an attack in the chapter "Weak Points and Strong." He pointed out that one should gather all the strong forces for an attack. Military tactics are like unto water, shaping its course according to different geography. To achieve this, an army must consolidate its strategy and fully master the war tactics. One of my principles at work is to fully understand the underlying logic and structure first, no matter what task I take on, so that I can adapt to changes. Perhaps it is because of this that my colleagues think I can cope with most situations.

This seemingly extraordinary skill was also born out of repeated practices in ordinary matters. If there was anything extraordinary, it would be making the effort to practice every day for over ten years.

We all have different understandings of matters and thus have different reactions. Having worked at CNOOD for 10 years, both my working and living environments have undergone great changes, but what remains unchanged is that I am still an ordinary person living

净、舒适就行，只是因为职务变化，要见更多的人 / 参与更多场合，着装也随之变得更正式、更体面，加之太太对我的贴心关照，衣服数量和款式增多，但我日常还是习惯只穿那几件。人的精力有限，更多时候我们需要聚焦在自己价值观系统中最重要的那几个部分。

4. 承认普通是常态，接纳普通是心态

过普通人的普通生活，这样的态度如今也迁移到我的育儿理念中。

2021年，我的女儿出生了。初为父母，我和太太自然也经历了对孩子未来的设想和考量这个过程。但回归到现实，我更多思考的是，如何让孩子从小就能有过好普通人一生的基本能力。比如，如何拥有面对困境依然能够乐观微笑的能力？在面对普通生活时，如何能够以坚韧的心性耐得住孤独寂寞的能力？

我认为，在生命的起始阶段，如果可以给到孩子这样的培养或影响，那么自家这个普通的孩子在过普通的人生时，能够

an ordinary life. Take something as trivial as choosing clothes as an example. Before, when my living conditions were not that good, I did not care too much about my dress, as long as the clothes were wearable, clean, and comfortable. Now, my attitude remains the same. Promoted to a higher position, I now possess many more formal and decent clothes in various styles, many bought by my wife for me to wear to different occasions and meet different people. However, what I am most accustomed to are still those same old items of clothing. With limited energy, we need to mostly focus on our most important values.

IV. Admitting Ordinariness Is Normality, While Accepting Ordinariness Is Mentality

Be an ordinary person who lives an ordinary life. This attitude is also reflected in my parenting philosophy now.

In 2021, my daughter was born. As first-time parents, naturally, my wife and I also tried to envision our daughter's future and evaluate her every possible path. But back to reality, what I care more about is how she can develop the basic ability to live an ordinary life well. For example, how to remain optimistic even in the face of difficulties? In an ordinary life, how to be resilient enough to endure the loneliness?

I believe that if parents can nurture or influence their kids in this aspect in their early stages of life, then there will be

感受幸福的概率就会变大吧。这比教育环境有多好，成绩有多棒更重要。在如今纷繁复杂的教育形势下，作为父亲有这样的理念，大概率会被认为是不太负责任的。

说实话，为人父母，未必拥有比孩子更好的承受力。同时，我充分地认识到父母和子女的关系，不是高级生命带领低级生命前进，而也许是智慧的给予者和接受者之间的心传。如果能够这么做当然很好，不过在带孩子的过程中，我发现很难做到这一点。作为父母，为孩子创造一个比较稳定和宽松的成长环境，这是有可能的；引导孩子避免一些原则性错误，也是有可能的。

所以，我们能做的更多是调整好自己的心态，做好一个花盆，然后等着种子慢慢发芽成长。总想着自己亲自上手，教会种子怎么长叶片、开什么形状的花才最美，可能并非双方之福，反而很大程度上限制了孩子的可能性。

如今，由于职务和家庭原因，我出差的时间越来越少，大部分时间都是公司和家两点一线，下了班就回家带女儿或休息，不吸烟，不嗜好饮酒，没有太多社交

a greater chance that the kids feel happy when they grow up to lead ordinary lives. This is more important than having a favorable education environment and getting good grades. However, against today's complex and convoluted education landscape, it would probably be considered too irresponsible for a father to hold such a philosophy.

To be honest, as parents, we do not necessarily have a higher degree of tolerance. Meanwhile, I am fully aware that the interactions between parents and kids are not seniors leading juniors, but perhaps heart-to-heart communications that transmit wisdom. It would of course be great if this could be achieved, but I find it quite hard when bringing up my kids. However, as parents, it should be possible to create for kids a relatively stable and relaxing environment. It should also be possible for parents to provide guidance so that their kids won't blunder on fundamental principles.

Therefore, what we can do is more about adjusting our mentality. It's like making a flower pot and waiting for the seeds to gradually germinate and grow. If you always try to get your own hands on the seedlings and teach them how to grow leaves or what shapes their flowers should take, none will be benefitted in the end, with your kids' potentials restricted.

Now, because of my new position and the need to take care of my family, I do not go on business trips as much, and most of the time, I only commute back

活动，也没有特别痴迷的爱好，偶尔在太太和女儿入睡后，我会打打游戏，看看新闻或网文。作为"90后"，我这样的生活大概会被评价为"苦行僧"，或者还会有人惋惜，说结了婚、生了娃就生不由己，可我却觉得这就是普通人的生活，知足且乐在其中。

人的大脑可以装得下世界，但人的心要忠于自己，充分认知自己，围绕自己内心的平衡点处事，向下扎根，向上生长，以普通人的心态过有度的人生。

and forth between company and home every day.

Having no obsessions such as smoking, drinking, or networking, I directly go back home to accompany my daughter or take a rest after work. Occasionally, when my wife and daughter are asleep, I will play some video games or read some news or online literature. For members of the post-90s generation, such a life would be commented as too "ascetic." Some might sigh that this is how life springs out of control after getting married and having a baby. But for me, this is what an ordinary life is like. I feel content and enjoy it very much.

We can put the whole world into our mind, but deep in our heart, we must remain loyal to and fully understand ourselves to find inner balance. Being pragmatic while aiming high, we can live a moderate life with the mentality of an ordinary person.

魏 坤
Andy Wei

在施璐德亚洲有限公司工作超十年老员工，新晋奶爸。爱国、爱党、爱群众、爱公司，爱家庭。

A veteran who has been working at CNOOD for more than ten years and a new dad, Andy loves the country, the Party, the people, the company and his family.

CNOOD 十年，我的十年
My Ten Years at CNOOD

■ Belinda Chen

2012年10月23日，我正式加入CNOOD公司，距今刚好十年，如今也能自豪的说一句：我也算是CNOOD的老员工了。

我与CNOOD相识是冥冥中的缘分。本科毕业后，我就直接进入职场，在宝山的钢贸公司工作了三年。对于一个刚毕业、怀揣冲劲儿的应届毕业生来说，那里的工作相对安逸，生活和大学校园类似，简简单单，轻松自在，但三年的成长相对缓慢。当我在犹豫该如何选择以后的方向的时候，身边两位朋友不约而同地都推荐了CNOOD，说是命中注定的缘分也不为过了。

我至今还记得面试时，池总问我未来五年和十年的规划。一个还没真正体验过职场拼搏的菜鸟，要畅想未来五年和十年，有点难，有种身处阴霾拨不开

On October 23, 2012, I joined CNOOD. That was exactly ten years ago. Now, I can also proudly proclaim that I am a veteran at CNOOD.

Getting to know CNOOD felt like destiny for me. After graduating from college, I directly entered the workforce and found a job at a steel material trading company in Baoshan. I worked there for three years, which felt a bit too easy and comfortable for a fresh graduate determined to fight for the future. Life there was like college campus life, simple and relaxing, but with relatively slow personal growth. Just as I dithered over my future development path, it happened that two of my friends both recommended CNOOD to me. It would not be an exaggeration to say that it was fate.

I still vividly remember my interview with Dennis, who asked about my plans for the next five years and ten years. As a rookie who had yet to truly wrestle at

闯不过的迷茫，甚至池总铺设的蓝图也让我觉得有点不敢想象，但这次的职业选择却在无意中为我打开了一扇充满未知的神秘之门。

进入 CNOOD 第一天，我的生活就发生了天翻地覆的变化，好像一下子被注入了能量，每一天都在经历着人生中的第一次：一个人租房子，一个人生活，一个人做饭。在适应新工作的同时，也要适应新的生活环境和方式，有些兵荒马乱，但对未知生活充满了好奇。CNOOD 的同事相处起来简单融洽，每个人都很上进，从不存在有人积极、有人摸鱼的分化状态。

在这里，学会独立是很重要的，你独立的程度决定了你能走多远，也决定了你是否能和团队一起打持久战。上班第二天，我就被派去出差，听到安排的一瞬间不禁一头雾水，大脑里反复闪过一句话：在公司我还是个新人，真的要我去吗？风险会不会太大了？后来我才知道这就是 CNOOD 的企业风格，欢迎新人最好的方式就是直接把你放在"战场"上，在实战中"练兵"，在事上打磨，在项目中锤炼。工作一段时间后，想起面试时池总说的话，隐隐觉得，这蓝图好像也不是不能实现。

work, it was hard to picture the next five or ten years. I felt as if lost in a haze, and even the blueprint that Dennis laid out for me seemed too good to imagine. However, inadvertently, this career choice opened for me a door to the uncharted mystery.

My life became completely different the moment I started working at CNOOD, as if there was energy injected all of a sudden. Every day, I would be experiencing some lifetime firsts: renting an apartment on my own, living on my own, and cooking on my own, all for the first time. Adapting to the new living environment, new lifestyle, as well as the new work, I was a bit overwhelmed, but brimming with curiosity at the same time. My colleagues at CNOOD are all easy-going and motivated, with no one slacking off.

Here, learning to be independent is very important. How independent you are determines how far you can go and whether you can work together with colleagues to fight protracted battles. On my second day on the job, I was sent on a business trip. I was baffled when I heard the news and could not help but wonder whether it was wise to give me, a rookie, such an important assignment. Wouldn't it be too big a risk? It was only later that I came to understand that this was the way at CNOOD to welcome newcomers, which was to send them straightly to the battlefield so that they could get trained and refine themselves directly through

十年后的今天，再次回想起当年池总描绘的蓝图，内心早已淡定如常。毕竟，时间和成果已经在不断告诉我，池总是一个有本事造梦，又能让梦想变成现实的企业家。CNOOD 在他的带领下，已经从一家小贸易公司转型为极速发展的跨国企业，如果非要用什么来形容，我会把 CNOOD 比作一艘宇宙飞船，一艘以无限探索为使命的宇宙飞船。

1. 在 CNOOD，一切的不可能都有可能

刚进公司时，池总的处事风格给我留下非常深刻的印象。那时公司正面临一家企业的索赔。十年前，一般的贸易公司在面对客户恶意索赔时，或者拒绝，或者采取各种手段维权。但池总二话没说，直接做了赔付，一个刚起步不久的公司，老板居然有这样的魄力，时隔十年，我依然还记得自己当时内心的感受：震撼，更敬佩！

practices and real projects. After working at CNOOD for a period of time, recalling what Dennis said at the interview, I had an inkling that the blueprint he laid out was not unthinkable after all.

Today, ten years later, when I once again recall that blueprint, it no longer sounds like a wonder to me. After all, the past ten years and all our achievements have demonstrated to me that Dennis is indeed an entrepreneur who has the ability to create dreams and then make those dreams come true. Under his leadership. CNOOD has grown from a small trading company to a fast-growing multinational enterprise. If anything, I would compare CNOOD to a spaceship, taking on the mission to make endless explorations.

Ⅰ. At CNOOD, All Impossibilities Are Possible

When I first joined the company, one thing left me with a deep impression regarding how Dennis handled disputes. At that time, CNOOD was facing a claim from another enterprise. Ten years ago, when faced with a malicious claim, an ordinary trading company generally would refuse to pay or take various methods to safeguard its legal rights. However, Dennis did not fight back and went straight ahead to make the payment. How courageous and decisive it was for the boss of a new start-up to make such a decision! Even after ten years, I could still vividly recall the shock and respect I felt

后来我才明白，与其花时间在这样的事情上拉扯，不如多花点精力在项目上，既维护了公司形象，也节省了时间和精力。那时是 2012 年，我相信就算放在 2022 年，这样的人也很少见。遇到利益纠纷，每个人都会从自己的角度去权衡，更要仔细斟酌，以免吃亏。但池总却教我们舍九存一，要始终锚定在最重要的事情上。这是我来到公司后上的第一课。

除此之外，CNOOD 的管理制度手册上还写明，鼓励员工去学习深造。我算是公司比较早的一批去考 MBA 的，原本是想考一个周末班，这样既不耽误工作，也可以学习充电。

但后来在办公室聊天时，我随口提了一句：全日制的 MBA 毕业后可以在上海落户。池总听到后很自然地接了一句：那你怎么不报全日制班呢？紧接着，他帮我写了推荐信，这样我面试通过的概率就更大了，只需要安心复习准备笔试。如果不是池总的一句话，我可能就选择读周末班，也不会有这么沉浸式的学习体验。那时候我刚组建了家庭，读书期间又恰逢孕期，一边工作，一边读书，一边待产，每天的生活忙碌而充实。

at that time.

It was only later that I came to realize that it was not worth it to waste time on such trivial matters, and it would be much more worthwhile to put our efforts into real projects. This way, we have spared our time and efforts, while also maintaining the company image. It was 2012 then, but even if in 2022, I believe few would have done what Dennis did. When interests are at stake, everyone will weigh up their options from their own perspectives to avoid losses. However, Dennis taught us to shed the insignificant 90% and focus on the important 10%. This was the first lesson I learned at CNOOD.

Besides, CNOOD wrote in its management system manual that employees are encouraged to pursue further education. I was among the first at CNOOD to apply for MBA programs. Initially, I planned to apply for a part-time MBA program so that it would not affect my work when I attend the program.

But later, when we were chatting in the office, I casually mentioned that a full-time MBA graduate would be qualified to register for permanet residence in Shanghai. Without hesitation, Dennis cut in, "Then why don't you apply for a full-time program?" Without delay, he wrote me a recommendation letter to enhance my chance of passing the interview so that I could focus on preparing for the written exam. If it wasn't for Dennis's reassurance, I might have chosen to attend

回忆这十年，我人生中的几件大事，都是在 CNOOD 完成的，很多在旁人眼中看来不可能的事，在 CNOOD 就是实实在在地发生了。

2. 在 CNOOD，每一天都是创业者的状态

我刚进 CNOOD 时，公司的业务板块并不大，我跟着 Fay 姐一起跟进一部分南美项目，后来业务逐渐扩展到中东、非洲等地，眼看着板块越做越大，在见证了公司转型和飞速发展的同时，我的工作也变得越来越忙，很多时候不能照顾到家庭，职场女性工作和家庭如何平衡的问题一度成为我的困扰。当时，家人觉得我很辛苦，提出让我考虑换一份工作，离家近，可以照顾孩子，哪怕赚得少一点。

先生的期盼和孩子在成长期对妈妈的需求，让我也考虑过换工作，但静下来后又问自己：离开了 CNOOD 我能去哪儿？我应该往哪儿走？CNOOD 在转型动荡期我都坚守下来了，如今真的要离开吗？工

a part-time program and would not have had the immersive learning experience of a full-time program. At that time, I just got married, and then got pregnant after I was admitted. Between all the work and study, while also expecting a baby, every day was busy but fulfilling.

Looking back on the past ten years, several of my major life events took place at CNOOD. What seemed impossible to others indeed happened at CNOOD.

Ⅱ. At CNOOD, Every Day, It Feels Like Starting Up

When I first joined CNOOD, it did not have a big business sector. Together with Fay, I followed up on some projects in South America. Then we gradually expanded our business to the Middle East and Africa. While witnessing the growth of the sector and the transformation and rapid development of our company, I became increasingly busy at work and did not have enough time to attend to my family. I was plagued by the same issue facing many women in the workplace—how to balance work and family. At that time, my family members thought that I was overworking myself and suggested that I find a new job closer to home so that I could take care of the kids, even if it would mean a lower salary.

My husband's expectations and my kids, demand for maternal care led me to consider the option of finding a new job. But then I asked myself, "Where can I go if I leave CNOOD? Which

作和家庭就真的这么难兼顾吗?

其实,我想很多同事都和我有一样的心情,不是离开CNOOD就不能生存,而是离开这里,很难再遇到这样的平台。

CNOOD的机制是多元化的,所以公司无论从管理、时间还是项目处理上,都给予同事最大的自由度,我们有机会自己把握今天该做什么,明天可以做什么,根据自己的节奏来做事情,很少有公司能给予这么大的权限。同时,在这里的每一个人都是有极强内驱力的,不要领导和同事督促。在这里,公司会给我们提供机会和资源,助我们开拓市场、完成项目。我们不仅仅是员工,更是创业者,每一天都在以创业者的状态奋斗。看起来好像个人时间少一点,但实际上可控性、可操作性还是比较强的。我很庆幸在毕业后不久就遇到了CNOOD,让我更快掌握自己做事的节奏,并能善于利用自己的优势来做事。

这样想来,我毫不犹豫地选择留在CNOOD。对我来说,家庭重要,事业同样重要,这里的工作让我有成就感和价值感。

direction should I take? I have stayed with CNOOD through its transformation and turbulences, should I really leave at this moment? Is it really that hard to balance work and family?"

In fact, I believe many of my colleagues feel the same. It is not that we cannot survive if we leave CNOOD, but that it will be extremely unlikely for us to encounter such a platform again.

CNOOD has a diversified mechanism, which gives employees as much leeway as possible, be it management, time control, or project handling. We have the opportunity to determine our own agenda for today and tomorrow and work at our own pace. Few companies entrust employees with such autonomy. Meanwhile, all the colleagues here are extremely self-motivated, requiring no supervision from superiors or colleagues. Here, CNOOD provides us with opportunities and resources and helps us expand markets and carry out projects. We are not only employees, but also entrepreneurs. Every day, we are fighting and striving like an entrepreneur. It seems as if there was less personal time, but actually, everything is rather controllable and operable. It was lucky for me that I joined CNOOD not long after graduation, which enabled me to develop my own pace of work and learn to fully leverage my strengths.

Thus, without any hesitation, I chose to stay at CNOOD. For me, family is important, but so is career. Working here makes me feel pride and fulfillment.

我们现在接触的项目，其实并没那么容易，不仅是谈项目，很多还会涉及技术问题，比如要会看图纸，看技术文件，因为所有项目都是国外的，我们甚至还要去消化西语资料。这些有难度，都需要跳一跳才能够得着。从个人角度来讲，确实偶尔会觉得艰难，但最后能想办法克服掉，就会像打了胜仗一样兴奋。

除此之外，CNOOD 的工作氛围也让我很喜欢，每一个项目从立项到收尾都有团队在背后支撑。有些项目体量大，每个人分摊下来工作都不少，在关键时刻依据各自的优势来适时补位。团队成员之间取长补短、相互协助，遇事有人商量、有人支持，给足了团队协助的安全感。在这样的环境下，越是高压状态，越能激发我们

The projects we are working on now are not easy. We not only need to carry out negotiations but also need to gain some technical knowledge because we have to read drawings and review technical documents. All our projects are overseas, making it necessary for us to digest even Spanish materials. All these tasks are difficult and cannot be accomplished without efforts. From a personal perspective, it is true that we sometimes feel difficult, but in the end, all the difficulties can be overcome, and we will feel very excited, as if winning a battle.

In addition, I also enjoy the working environment at CNOOD, where there is a team providing support for each project from inception to completion. Some projects are of such a large volume that each team member is assigned with plenty of tasks. At critical moments, we also need to take on new tasks according

的斗志，在一次次的胜利中体会到团队作战的酣畅淋漓。很难的事情克服掉了，又中了一个项目，得到了客户的认可……那种不断冲锋、不断攻克堡垒的状态让人享受。

其实CNOOD有时候很像一个巨型的创业孵化器，让每一位同事都能有创业者的状态，并时刻保持冲锋的敏锐。这十年来，我并不是进步最大、发展最快的，但我的状态较稳，踏踏实实推进项目，遇到机会从不放弃，积极想办法解决问题。我想，我早已经有了作为CNOOD人该有的灵魂。在CNOOD，永远不必着急，只要你准备好想做什么，公司一定会有相应的资源和机会让你去做这件事。

3. 每一次成长都伴随阵痛

2021年，我工作上遇到了一次蜕变。从2014年就开始对接的客户终于直接签上了合同（原先只是间接通过其他公司合作）。长达七年的客户跟进，我经历了每次投标都石沉大海、毫无音讯的过程，曾

to each member's merits. Team members can draw on each other's strengths, assist, consult and support each other, and create a safety net of team collaboration. In such an environment, the more pressure we feel, the more motivated we are, savouring the thrill of teamwork through each victory. Overcoming a difficulty, winning a bid, gaining the recognition of a client ... We really enjoy the state of constantly charging and conquering the fortress.

Sometimes, CNOOD is really like a huge start-up incubator, allowing every colleague to maintain the spirit of entrepreneurship and the acuteness in pioneering. Over the past decade, I was not the employee with the biggest progress and the fastest development, but I have maintained a relatively steady progress, advancing projects step by step, never giving up any opportunity, and always taking the initiative to solve problems. I believe that I have already cultivated my CNOOD spirit. At CNOOD, there is no need to worry. The company definitely has the resources and opportunities you need, as long as you are prepared.

III. Every Growth Is Accompanied by Pain

In 2021, I went through a metamorphosis in my work. I finally managed to sign a contract directly with a client that I have been working with since 2014 (before this, we only cooperated indirectly through

经想过放弃、想过退缩，甚至有过自我怀疑。2016—2020 年，这样的内耗导致这个客户的项目在不同同事中间流转，迟迟未出结果。2020 年底，Fay 姐再次问我是否还想继续跟进这个客户的时候，我迟疑了，甚至内心有点抵触。曾经花了那么多时间去跟进却始终没有结果，再接触也不知道值不值得。就在想打退堂鼓的时候，Fay 姐适时推了我一把。困难这回事，就怕坚持，一旦坚持下来，其实也就没那么可怕了。

标书一投，也并不是立竿见影，后面又花了好几个月才终于拿到合同。看到中标的反馈，心里五味杂陈，历时多年，成功早已不是喜悦能言说的，毕竟中标并不是结果，只是万里长征的第一步，后面能够顺利沟通并交付才是关键。果不其然，交付期间不仅要配合客户的时间倒时差开会，还需要克服语言障碍。这个项目比较复杂，从设计、生产到检验，要事无巨细地跟客户沟通，无论是开会还是发邮件，都需要用西语来沟通，一边做项目一边还要克服语言问题。

other companies). During seven long years of follow-up, every bid we placed saw no response at all. I also considered giving up once, recoiling and even doubting myself. From 2016 to 2020, because this process was too self-consuming, the project was handed over to one colleague after another, without any result delivered. By the end of 2020, when Fay asked me again whether I still wanted to follow up with this client, I hesitated, feeling even a hint of resistance. With so much time already put in but without any result, I did not know whether it would be worthwhile to maintain contact with the client. Just as I was considering drawing back, Fay encouraged me in due time. Difficulties would back off in the face of perseverance; as long as you hold on, the obstacles will no longer seem so formidable.

After placing the bid, I waited another several months before finally winning the contract. When I saw the news that we won the bid, a myriad of feelings overwhelmed me. After so many years of effort, what success brought me was much more than pure happiness. After all, winning the bid was not the final stop, but only the first step toward a 10-thousand-mile journey, where smooth communication and delivery would be the key. Indeed, during the phase of delivery, we had to cope with our time difference with the client and hold conferences according to the client's schedule. We also had to overcome the language barrier.

就这么经历了近两年的时间，算是狠狠蜕了一层皮，但也把自己历炼到了一个新阶段，再遇到类似的客户，我也可以轻松自如的应对。现在想来，很感谢 Fay 姐，在我想退缩的时候出来推动我向前多走一步。其实，面对客户也好，面对自己的人生也好，有时候就需要这么一步，跨过去了，能力就提升一档。我们要做的，就是接纳和面对。

2022 年疫情期间，我刚好在国外出差，国外的防控措施没那么严格，我在工作期间不幸中招，当即自我隔离。生病，身处异国他乡，再加上不太顺利的客户沟通，连番打击，让我一贯平平稳稳的心态被击碎，甚至导致我情绪爆发。然而，不轻言放弃的性格让我在经历低谷之后重新去审视当时的状态以及自己以后的方向。

The project was relatively complicated, and we needed to go over every detail with the client throughout the whole process of design, production, and inspection. All communications, be it conferences or emails, were conducted in Spanish, and we had to hone our language skills while delivering the project.

This process went on for nearly two years, and I felt like shedding a layer of skin, which also pushed me to refine my skills and reach a new level. In the future, I would be able to cope with similar clients with ease. Now looking back, I am very grateful that Fay pushed me forward while I cowered. In fact, whether facing clients or obstacles in our own life, sometimes what is needed is just that one more step; if you take that step, your abilities will be raised to the next level. What we need to do is to accept and confront the challenges.

During the 2022 epidemic, I happened to be on a business trip abroad. The epidemic control measures there were not as strict, and I caught COVID while working there. I immediately went into self-isolation, which, added to the pains of being sick, the loneliness of being overseas, and the less-than-smooth client communication, shattered my usually stable mood and led to an emotional breakdown. However, I was not a person who would give up easily, which allowed me to re-examine my state of mind and my future direction even at my lowest ebb.

其实，经历过了就觉得当时的种种就只是经历，是一种置之死地而后生的难得的人生体验。站在当下只觉得收获、感悟更多。

CNOOD 一直是团队作战，几年项目做下来，我最大的感受是，很多事情做了，还有希望；不做，就一点机会都没了。如果每次都以望而生畏收场，那放弃就会变成习惯。遇到难题，要先想着怎么解决。

In effect, having gone through all these, now I see the hardships only as precious life experience, where what doesn't kill me makes me stronger. Now, what I draw from that experience is only fulfillment and inspiration.

At CNOOD, we always work in teams. After several years of delivering projects, my biggest takeaway is that in many situations, if you take action, there is still hope, but if you don't, there will be no chance left. If you flinch from difficulties every time, then giving up will become a habit. With an obstacle ahead, your first thought should be about how to remove it.

做越难的事情，就越能激发潜力，激发自己的隐藏力量。很多时候你并不知道自己的能量有多强、能力有多大，这需要在一个特定的环境中去检验。什么是特定的环境？就是高压、困境。在这其中，才能激发整个人的潜力。这种环境会有，职场多年总会遇到，但从机会的角度来说，非常难得。现在很多职场人有畏难心理，会选择在自己的舒适圈里做事，这样可能会保一时口碑，但对成长和发展都不太有利。

有人问我，在接这些在当时看起来没太大把握的任务时会恐惧吗？

说实在的也会有，但是我一直相信一句话：简单就是力量。我先生一直说我的想法比较简单，做一件事很少会畏首畏尾，遇到事第一反应是接纳，第二就是思考如何解决，该怎么做就怎么做。有时候把事情想得太复杂，反而让自己失去了很多机会。把注意力放在内耗上和把注意力放在成事上，最后的结果一定是不同的。我自小的成长环境很简单，一座小城镇，身边的人也没那么复杂，"该做什么就做什么"是我长大过程中听过最多的话。

The more difficult your task is, the more potential you will be able to uncover. Oftentimes, you do not know your strength, which needs to be tested in a certain environment. What is such an environment? It would involve high pressure and difficulties. Only in such an environment can you tap your full potential. Such situations do exist, but rare. After years of work, inevitably, you will be faced with one such environment, which will be a very precious opportunity. Now, many staff in the workplace fear difficulties and choose to stay in their comfort zones, which may keep their reputation in the short term, but will not benefit their growth and development in the long run.

I was once asked whether I would feel afraid when taking on tasks where I do not have enough self-confidence.

Honestly, I would. But I always believe in the saying that simplicity is power. My husband always say that I think in a straightforward way, without excessive fears or misgivings; when I meet with a difficulty, I always accept it straight away, think about how to solve the problem, and then do what I have to do. Sometimes, dwelling on the complexities will only cost you a lot of opportunities. Consuming yourself with worries and fears and focusing on delivering results will definitely lead to different outcomes. I grew up in a simple small town without complex relations. "Do what you have to do" was the saying that came up most

另外，我也从不会给自己设限。一般人都会给自己设定一个很明确的限制——我能做到哪里。我不会。虽然有些事情我没做过，但是我相信通过自己的努力跳一跳也能够得着；即使自己不行，也可以借助外界力量来达成。无论是人际关系还是专业能力，或是他人的一个见解、建议，都是我可以去借助的力量。想要做到这一点，首先对自己的角色定位要足够清晰。比如我的定位就是开发不同的客户，让项目落地执行，这是我的主线，另外的支线就可以拆分出去，放在团队内部，大家彼此协作。

现在很多人不太懂得借力，或是对借力这种事会犹豫不决，他们会思考太多细节，权衡太多，但在CNOOD，彼此协作一直都是企业文化中的一条，更是我们的核心。懂得借力的人，是有清晰愿景和规划的人。

总之，站在当下回看过去，感谢自己当时选择继续，选择了坚持，到如今才有了不同的人生阅历，毕竟人没有办法用当下的视角去评判过去的事，只能庆幸自己没放弃，也庆幸身边有领导和同事的推动和支持，才有了那个当下所做的最好的决定。

frequently when I grew up.

Besides, I never set limits for myself. People often set a clear limit for themselves, delimiting the ceiling of their ability. I don't. Though for some things I have never tried, I believe that through my efforts, I can accomplish the tasks. Even if I cannot do it on my own, I can still lean on outside assistance, such as interpersonal relations, professional capabilities, and others' opinions and suggestions. To achieve this, one must first have clear self-positioning. For me, my main task is to develop new clients and implement projects, so other sideline tasks can be assigned to other team members, achieving collaboration.

Now, many people don't know how to seek assistance or dither over this, dwelling on too many details and weighing up different options. However, at CNOOD, collaboration has always been ingrained in and at the core of our corporate culture. Those who know how to seek assistance are those with clear visions and plans.

In all, looking back, I am truly grateful that I chose to persevere and charge ahead at that time, leading to the life experiences I have now. No one can judge the past based on the current perspective. It was really fortunate that I did not give up and had the encouragement and support from superiors and colleagues so that I could make the best choice.

4. 关于未来？过好每一天，就是未来

疫情期间，我们每个人都绷着一根弦，不知道什么时候会有变数发生。如今政策放开，国内外通行，接下来如果有假期可以自行支配，我会选择出去旅行，去一直让自己心驰神往的地方，比如新疆、西藏，都是让我觉得神秘又想探索的地方。

我很喜欢去感受不同的东西，去见见不同的人、不同的环境，体会不同的文化。

以前工作的时候曾经去过迈阿密和伊斯坦布尔，我很喜欢那里。现在还记得当时工作之余在迈阿密的海边吹海风，内心很平静。而伊斯坦布尔则富有宗教色彩，那里的清真寺、特殊的餐饮都给我留下深刻的印象。去不同地域旅行，见天地，是挺有意思的事。

除此之外，我想新的一年，也要学习如何更好地与家里的两个"小魔头"相处。孩子越来越大，亲子沟通和互动变得更重要。每次出差回来先生都会反馈，我在家和不在家，孩子的表现是很不一样。我想，他们还小，即使日常和我相处起来鸡飞狗跳，但我们彼此的心里是惦记对方的，是有爱的。未来我依旧还是无暇给他们讲故事，甚至无暇陪伴，但我会在他们需要我时，及时给予拥抱，并把爱表达出

IV. About Future? Future Is Just Living Each Day Well

During the epidemic, we were all on tenterhooks, uncertain when a bad news would hit. Now that the COVID control measures are loosened and we can travel freely at home and abroad, for the next vacation at my disposal, I will choose to travel to some places that have always fascinated me, such as Xinjiang and Tibet, both mysterious places that I want to explore.

I enjoy feeling different things, meeting different people, experiencing different environments, and encountering different cultures.

I had once been to Miami and Istanbul on business trips. I loved those places. I still remember enjoying the sea breezes on the beaches in Miami in my leisure time, feeling the tranquility of my mind. Istanbul had more religious touches, with all the mosques and specialty foods leaving me a deep impression. Travelling to different places broadens my horizon and brings me enormous joy.

Apart from this, in the new year, I want to learn to better get along with my two "little devils." As they grow older, parent-child communication and interactions become even more important. Every time I come back from a business trip, my husband will tell me that the kids behave differently when I am not around. I think, while young, and while our interactions are often full of quarrels

来。其实，孩子的包容度比我们想象得要多。

在 CNOOD 这十年，让我体会到无论做妈妈，做妻子，还是做三头六臂的职场人，这原本就是一生的修行。所以，别急，慢慢来。下一个十年，在 CNOOD 的带领下，相信我会收获更加绽放的自己。

and disputes, in the end, they still love and care about me, just as vice versa. In the future, I still might sometimes be too busy to read to them or accompany them, but when they need me, I will do my best to give them a timely hug and express my love for them. In fact, kids can tolerate a lot more than we think.

My past decade at CNOOD has taught me that it is a lifelong practice to learn to be good mother, a good wife, and a versatile employee. So, don't hurry, and take it easy. Following the lead of CNOOD, I believe that I will enjoy an even more thriving ten years.

陈玲玲
Belinda Chen

2012 年加入施璐德大家庭；2014—2017 年一边工作一边完成上海财经大学 MBA 课程；积极乐观，不轻言放弃。

Joining the big family of CNOOD in 2012, Belinda completed her MBA course at Shanghai University of Finance and Economics (SUFE) while working for the company from 2014 to 2017. As an optimist, she never gives up easily.

新岁序开，同赴新程
——施璐德 2022 年度总结大会圆满落幕！

A New Year Begins with A New Journey Ahead
— The 2022 CNOOD Annual Summary Conference

■ CNOOD News

2023 年 1 月 6 日，施璐德亚洲有限公司 2022 年度总结大会于上海办公室隆重举行，全体员工通过线上或线下的方式参与此次大会。会议议程分为高管述职、表彰先进、董事长寄语。

On January 6, 2023, the 2022 Annual Summary Conference of CNOOD ASIA LIMITED was held in the Shanghai office, and all employees participated in the conference through online and offline

1. 高管述职

首先，高管团队就2022年度工作分别述职，并对2023年的工作做出了展望与规划。

CEO李燕飞女士主持并第一个述职，通过一个"家"的模型，阐明了CNOOD十年发展纲领与当下发展阶段、管理职能与业务发展、CNOOD与个人的关系。

approaches. The conference agenda was mainly divided into three parts, including executive reporting, recognition of outstanding employees, and Chairman's speech.

I. Executive Reporting

To begin with, the executive team reported on their work performance for the year 2022 and shared their visions and plans for the year 2023.

CEO Mrs. Fay Lee presided over the conference and gave an opening speech. Through a "home" model, she explained the relationships between CNOOD's ten-year development plan and the current development stage, between management functions and business development, and between CNOOD and individuals.

CEO 李燕飞女士作述职报告
CEO Mrs. Fay Lee gave her work report

CNOOD 十年发展纲领是指导公司发展的蓝本，模型头部的序言、愿景、战略和十年规划目标，值得所有员工齐心协力，共同努力去完成。当前公司的发展，正是依托于十年发展纲领中提到的内容，有些只是播下种子，有些已经发芽，有些正在开花，而有些已经成熟结果。各位员工虽职能不同，分工不同，但目标相同，在十年纲领的指导下，只需全力以赴，静待花开！

当下，基于一系列标准化、流程化的制度文件，公司已经初步完成了管理职能的基础建设，明确自己深耕的方向，接下来，公司要考虑如何进一步提升，尤其在专业化、服务精神和全局思维这三个重点方向。这将面临更大的挑战。在《业务发展部工作手册》的指导下，业务部门已经审批通过13份业务计划书，这13份业务计划书分属12个业务团队。未来，公司会全面支持这12个业务团队取得成功，并持续孵化可行的业务计划，发展优秀的合伙人、开立有效的分/子公司。管理职能服务并支撑业务发展，业务发展不断牵引管理职能持续提升，双管齐下，与时俱进。

The CNOOD ten-year development plan is the blueprint for guiding development. The preface, vision, strategy, and ten-year planning goals at the head of the model are worth all employees' joint efforts. The current development of the company is based on the contents of the ten-year development plan. Some are still seeds, some have already sprouted, some are blooming, and some have already matured and borne fruit. Although all employees perform different functions and complete different tasks, we have the same goal. Under the guidance of the ten-year plan, we just need to go all out and wait for the flowers to bloom!

At present, based on a series of standardized and procedural-systematized documents, we have completed the preliminary infrastructure construction of management functions and have clarified the direction that our company should delve into. Next, we need to consider how to further improve, especially in three critical areas, which are professionalism, service spirit, and global thinking. Thus comes greater challenges. Under the guidance of the *Business Development Department Work Manual*, the business department has approved 13 business plans from 12 different business teams. In the future, we will build solid foundation to underpin the success of these 12 business teams and continue to incubate feasible business plans, develop excellent partners, and establish productive

在 CNOOD 项目和团队中，个人得以成长，发展，自由选择角色、团队、发展方向、业务模式，最终实现个人的职业发展、人生价值。与此同时，在 CNOOD，个人与同事、合作伙伴、客户形成利益共同体、事业共同体、命运共同体。我们在这个共同的家里，共创、共治、共享，互相包容、互相成全、互相成就！

branches/subsidiaries. The management functions serve and support business development while business development continuously drives the sustained improvement of management functions. The interplay between management functions and business development creates synergistic effects and enables the company to keep up with the times.

In terms of CNOOD projects and teams, individuals can grow and develop, and are given the freedom to choose their roles, teams, development directions, and business models, thus ultimately achieving personal career development and realizing life value. At the same time, in CNOOD, individuals form a community of shared interests, career, and destiny with colleagues, partners, and clients. In this big family, we embrace mutual tolerance, mutual fulfillment, and mutual achievement through co-creating, co-governing, and sharing.

COO 丁林生先生作述职报告
COO Mr. Tiger Ding delivered his work report

接下来由 COO 丁林生先生述职，就"全年业务概况、部门建设、2023 年工作计划"等方面做了全面细致的梳理。

2022 年，外部环境相当困难。2022 年，公司在内部管理尤其是职能部门建设方面快速推进，取得比较明显的成效。

2022 年，新签订单量和营业收入等指标均呈上升势头。除了传统业务基本盘稳健发展外，公司在新模式、新领域方面有多项突破。

2022 年的成绩来之不易，海外疫情尚未褪去，海外生产和施工在逆境中推进。但在大家同心协力下，都出色完成了。

2023 年，一方面，外部环境会有较大变化，业务部门要抓住机遇期，更多走出去，贴近市场，加大客户的服务范围延伸和核心领域的客户延展。另一方面，公司要积极推进新领域、新模式，谨慎操作，形成更多的业务中心和利润中心。

2023 年，公司在管理上要进一步优化，职能部门应服务于业务发展诉求，提升服务能力，强化协同能力，从工具箱变成百宝箱。

Next, Mr. Tiger Ding, COO, reported on his work and provided a comprehensive and detailed presentation on "annual business overview, department development, and 2023 work plan."

2022 endured a considerably tough external environment. In 2022, the company's internal management, especially the development of functional departments, has rapidly advanced and achieved significant results.

In 2022, indicators such as newly signed orders and business revenue showed an upward trend. In addition to the stable development of the company's traditional business fields, there have been multiple breakthroughs in new models and fields.

The achievements of 2022 were not easy, and the overseas pandemic has not yet subsided. Overseas manufacturing and construction have advanced against the headwind. But with everyone's concerted efforts, all turned out well.

In 2023, the external environment will be greatly changed, and business teams should seize this opportunity to go out, stay close to the market, extend the scope of customer service, and develop more clients for the company's core businesses. On the other hand, we should actively promote new fields and models, operate in a cautious manner, and form more business centers and profit centers.

In 2023, management will be further optimized. Functional departments will better serve business development needs, enhance service capabilities, strengthen

丁林生先生强调，每个员工要心存CNOOD的发展理念与企业文化，做自己职业上的主人。

之后，总工程师张林先生基于2022年度部门工作总结，阐述了2023年工作规划。

2022年，公司的设计和技术管理工作逐步走向流程化和规范化，通过业务交流会和管理团队月度例会，我们更好地了解了公司业务对设计和技术的需求，加强了设计和技术层面对公司业务的支持力度。

collaborative capabilities, and turn toolboxes into treasure boxes.

Mr. Tiger Ding emphasized that everyone should be the master of their own profession with CNOOD philosophy and culture in mind.

Then, Mr. Lin Zhang, Chief Engineer, elaborated on the 2023 work plan based on the summary of the department's work during 2022.

In 2022, the company's design and technical management has become more process-based and standardized. Through business communication meetings and monthly management-level team meetings, we better understood the company's business requirements for design and technology and strengthened our support in design and technology for the company's business.

C.E 张林先生作述职报告
Chief Engineer Mr. Zhang Lin gave his work report

2022年，公司更加广泛地参与了海外项目投标报价，项目分布到卡塔尔、波兰、荷兰、意大利、俄罗斯、智利、秘鲁等国家和地区，专业涉及码头、桥梁、储罐、模块、污水处理、钢结构厂房、房建等领域，为实现公司十年规划目标开启了一个良好的局面。2022年，BIM技术、P6计划软件在项目投标工作中的应用，提升了投标文件的水平，增强了与客户的沟通效果，锻炼了人才队伍。

2023年，海外工程业务机会将会越来越多，业务类型也会更加多样化。我们要做好设计和技术资源的提前储备，加强服务意识，围绕业务拓展核心，全面做好设计和技术的支持、协同工作。为了满足不断增长的业务量需求，设计和技术专业人员要加强学习，提升我们的专业水平和管理能力，同时做好人才引进和新人培养工作，建立一个高水平、高效率的设计和技术团队。

CFO张召环先生因疫情影响，无法抵达现场，于线上进行述职总结，全面汇报

In 2022, the company participated more extensively in bidding and quotation of overseas projects, which were located in countries and regions such as Qatar, Poland, the Netherlands, Italy, Russia, Chile, and Peru. The projects required professional knowledge about piers, bridges, tanks, modules, sewage treatment, steel structure factories, and housing construction, marking a good start for achieving the company's 10-year planning goals. In 2022, the application of BIM technology and P6 planning software in project bidding has improved the quality of bidding documents, enhanced communication with customers, and upskilled the talent team.

In 2023, there will be more and more opportunities for overseas engineering business, and the types of business activities will become more diverse. We need to accumulate design and technical resources in advance, strengthen service awareness, expand core businesses, and comprehensively support and coordinate the provision of design and technology. In order to meet the demands of the constantly growing business volume, design and technical professionals need to strengthen their learning and improve our professional level and management ability. We also need to focus on talent acquisition and new talent cultivation and establish a high-level and efficient design and technical team.

Mr. Zhaohuan Zhang, CFO, was unable to attend the conference on site due

CFO 张召环先生作述职报告
CFO Mr. Zhaohuan Zhang delivered his work report

2022年度财务工作完成情况及2023年工作安排。

2022年，得益于全体员工的努力付出，公司经营业绩总体呈稳步上升趋势。一直以来的坚持，让我们看到了胜利的曙光，亦为今后的业务发展注入信心和力量。

同时，在公司各业务部、各部门的通力配合下，财务部已完成2023年度预算工作，这将为公司决策提供更充实的依据。

to the pandemic. He conducted a report of his work online and comprehensively reported on the financial work for 2022 and the work arrangements for 2023.

In 2022, thanks to the hard work and dedication of all employees, the overall business performance of the company showed a steady upward trend. With continued perseverance, we saw the dawn of victory, boosting confidence and strength for our future business development.

At the same time, with the cross-department cooperation of the whole company, our financial department has developed the 2023 budget, which will

2023年，财务部还将进一步加强部门团队建设与人员管理工作，深化服务意识，提升沟通效率，共谋发展。

2. 表彰先进

在高管团队完成年度述职后，董事长池勇海博士及CEO李燕飞女士为2022年度在施璐德工作中表现突出者颁发荣誉证书，以表彰他们为施璐德做出的卓越贡献。

provide a more substantial basis for the company's decision-making.

In 2023, the financial department will further strengthen departmental team building and personnel management, deepen service awareness, improve communication efficiency, and seek common development.

II. Recognition of Outstanding Employees

After the executive reporting, Dr. Dennis Chi, the chairman, and Mrs. Fay Lee, CEO, awarded honorary certificates to outstanding performers at CNOOD this year, in recognition and commemoration of their remarkable contributions to CNOOD.

董事长池勇海博士为获奖员工颁发荣誉奖项 Chairman Dr. Dennis Chi presented an honorary award to the award-winning employee

CEO李燕飞女士为获奖员工颁发荣誉奖项 CEO Mrs. Fay Lee presented an honorary award to the award-winning employee

沈佳祺表示"首先很荣幸当选2022年度优秀员工，得到领导和同事们的认可，这是对过去一年的肯定，也是对新的一年的鼓励。

回首2022年，很多事情还历历在目。在疫情期间我坚持各项工作的有序开展，逐步建立健全公司的合规体系，保持与内部外部的沟通。这一切都离不开公司其他各个职能部门给予的支持和协助，没有他们的支持，就无法共同创建合规体系并保证合规管理运行。

展望2023年，仍旧是充满机遇和挑战的一年。但我相信我们仍会坚守初心，用更多的努力来提升和完善整个公司的体系。"

Johnson Shen said, "Firstly, it is an honor to be elected as Outstanding Employee of the Year 2022, recognized by the management team and colleagues. This is an affirmation of my work performance during the past year and also an encouragement for the year to come.

Looking back on 2022, many things are still vivid. During the pandemic, I continued to carry out various tasks effectively, gradually established and improved the company's compliance system, and maintained communication with internal and external parties. All of this could not have been achieved without the support and assistance provided by other functional departments of the company. Without their support, we could not have jointly created and ensured the operation of compliance management.

Looking ahead to 2023, it will still be a year full of opportunities and challenges. But I believe we will still stick to our original aspiration and put more efforts to improve and perfect the entire company's system."

"优秀员工奖"获奖者：沈佳祺
"Outstanding Employee Award" Winner: Johnson Shen

陈玲玲表示:"非常感谢大家的信任让我能获得这个优秀员工奖。放眼我们公司和我们团队,比我优秀的人比比皆是,因此我认为我是代表项目组团队和F组所有成员领的奖。

过去一年多来,我们经常因为项目加班到晚上10点11点,甚至还有凌晨四五点爬起来和客户开会的经历。每当项目上遇到比较棘手的谈判或者技术问题,我们大家都是一起思考、一起讨论,一起与客户沟通,没有大家的努力付出就没有今天的这个奖。

对于我个人而言,我也一直在不断地平衡工作、生活和学习,不断在做着各种取舍,能做到所谓的平衡少不了他人的付出,比如同事、家人。我很感恩能身处这样一个积极向上的团队中,大家互相包容、互相成就,朝着共同的理想和目标一起努力、一起奋斗。

总而言之,为了对得起这个优秀员工奖,新的一年我还需更加努力,争取更好的成绩。"

陈玲玲同时获得了10周年忠诚奖,她再次发表了感言:"一眨眼十年已过,

Belinda Chen said, "Thank you very much for your trust and granting me this Outstanding Employee Award. There are many people who are better than me in our company and our team, and I believe that I am receiving the award on behalf of the project team and all members of Group F.

Over the past year or so, we have often worked overtime on projects until after 10 or 11 p.m. and even had the experience of getting up at 4 or 5 a.m. to have meetings with clients. Whenever we encountered tricky negotiations or technical issues on a project, we all brainstormed together, discussed together, and communicated with clients together. Without everyone's hard work and dedication, I wouldn't have been able to receive this award today.

For me personally, I have been constantly balancing work, life, and study and constantly making various choices. Being able to achieve the so-called balance is accompanied by the efforts of others, such as colleagues and family. I am very grateful to be in such a positive and upward team, where everyone is tolerant of each other, cheers for and supports others' successes, and works together towards common ideals and goals.

In summary, to be worthy of this excellent employee award, I need to work harder and strive for better results in the new year."

Belinda Chen also received the 10th Anniversary Loyalty Award, and once

"优秀员工奖"获奖者：陈玲玲
"Outstanding Employee Award" Winner: Belinda Chen

董事长池勇海博士为获奖员工颁发"10周年忠诚奖"
Chairman Dr. Dennis Chi presented the "10th Anniversary Loyalty Award" to the award–winning employee

我仍然清晰地记得自己第一次来到施璐德办公室时的样子。十年来，我见证了公司的成长与变化，自己也从最初的只身一人到现在的四口之家，从原来的本科学历到现在的研究生学历，从奔三到了奔四的年纪，我成长了、成熟了，积累了不少经验，也收获了不少教训。这点点滴滴的成长都离不开施璐德的培养以及各位同事的支持与帮助。

魏坤也获得了10周年忠诚奖，他表示："我觉得这个奖项特别有意义。依旧清晰地记得十年前第一次步入施璐德，开

again gave a speech, "Ten years have passed in the blink of an eye, and I still vividly remember the first time I came to the CNOOD office. Over the past ten years, I have witnessed the growth and changes of the company, and at the same time, I have also gone from being alone at the beginning to having a family of four, from a bachelor to a master, from my thirties to my forties. I have grown and matured, accumulated a lot of experience, and learned many lessons. These growths cannot be separated from the cultivation by CNOOD and the support and assistance from colleagues.

The 10th Anniversary Loyalty Award winner Andy Wei said, "I think this award is particularly meaningful. I still vividly

启职业生涯的情景，回首望去，十年时间也就是一眨眼，但细细想来，十年时间里我也经历了很多。生活上，我完成了结婚生娃、读书安家的人生大事；工作上可以说历经风雨，但整体上而言是很幸运的，特别感谢教导我的老师们，特别珍惜和同事们的缘分，也特别期待听到新加入公司的同事们的 10 周年忠诚奖获奖感言。"

remember the scene when I first stepped into CNOOD ten years ago and started my career. Looking back, ten years was just a blink of an eye, but when I think about it carefully, I have experienced a lot in the past ten years. In life, I have completed the major life events of getting married, having a child, studying, and settling down. In work, I can say that I have gone through ups and downs, but overall, I am very fortunate, and I am particularly grateful to the mentors who have taught me. I cherish my encounters with my colleagues and look forward to hearing the 10th anniversary loyalty award speeches from my new colleagues."

"10 周年忠诚奖" 获奖者：魏坤
"10th Anniversary Loyalty Award " Winner: Andy Wei

感恩公司、感谢各位同事！新的十年已开启，我已从内心把自己清零，重新出发，迎接新的机遇与挑战。"

Thank you to the company and all my colleagues! The new decade has begun, and I have let go of the past from the bottom of my heart and am ready to start afresh to meet new opportunities and challenges."

"10周年忠诚奖"获奖者：陈玲玲
"10th Anniversary Loyalty Award" Winner: Belinda Chen

3. 董事长寄语

III. Chairman's Speech

在总结大会的最后环节，董事长池勇海先生做了关于共谱新篇章的讲话。

他表示，在2022年内忧外患的艰难境地之下，公司管理层联合各部门协同发力，依然做出有目共睹的成绩，值得肯定。

In the final session, Mr. Dennis Chi, the chairman, delivered a speech about the company's new chapter.

He stated that facing the difficult domestic and international situation in 2022, the company management team, in collaboration with various departments, still achieved remarkable results, which is worthy of recognition.

董事长池勇海博士发表讲话
Chairman Dr. Dennis Chi delivered a speech

谈及未来，他提出要重视"赛道的选择与角色的提升"，这个世界是瞬息万变的，唯有顺应外界的变化，主动变化，选择真正适用的赛道，方能确保自身始终行进在正确的轨道之中。

施璐德是一个共创、共治、共享的平台，以成就人、培养人为目标，这是公司不懈推崇的理念。他倡导每个人都能沉下来，不断提升，做最好的自己，成就自己的事业。

Looking ahead, he proposed to attach importance to the selection of lane and the improvement of personal roles. This world is ever-changing, and one can only adapt to external changes, take the initiative to embrace changes, and choose the truly suitable lane to be always on the right track.

CNOOD is a platform for co-creation, co-governance, and sharing, with the goal of cultivating successful individuals. This is the philosophy CNOOD tirelessly promotes, advocating that everyone can stay grounded, continuously improve, become the best version of themselves, and achieve their own career goals.

荣誉是自己给的,"希望大家都有遥不可及的梦想"。

2022年我们在艰难中前行,2023年我们依旧满怀热望,祝全体施璐德人在新的一年里,以奋发有为的精神状态,共赴新程,大展宏"兔"!

时间:2023年1月6日

Honor is self-acquired, "I hope everyone has great dreams."

In 2022, we moved forward amidst difficulties, and in 2023, we are still full of hope. I hope that all CNOODers will have vigorous and energetic spirits to embark on a new journey and achieve great success in the year to come!

Time: January 6, 2023

记施璐德"予她闪耀"秋日主题活动
The CNOOD Fall Themed Event of "Let Her Shine"

■ CNOOD News

2022年9月28日,施璐德学会"予她闪耀分会"秋日主题活动温暖上线。施璐德女士们身着纯净优雅蓝色系服装和Suki老师再次相聚,共同探讨关于女性不同年龄阶段的心路历程。

On September 28, 2022, the fall themed event of CNOOD Society "Let Her Shine" was held. Ladies of CNOOD, dressed in pure and elegant blue attire, met again with Teacher Suki to discuss the psychological journey of women at different stages of their lives.

1. 暖场

I. Warm–Up

2. 辩论

职场妈妈如何平衡家庭和职业？孩子优先还是自己更重要？寻找另一半，互补还是同频？活动中就当代女性热门话题分组进行探讨，持不同观点的两方激烈辩论，试图说服对方，互不相让，在一次次思想交锋中迸发出无限灵感，轻松热闹的气氛蔓延全场。

II. Debate Session

How do working mothers balance family and career? Prioritize children or themselves? Similar or complementary, what's the best partner? During the event, participants were asked to form different teams to discuss the hot topics faced by contemporary women. During intense debates between two sides with opposite viewpoints, they tried to persuade each other without compromise and received great inspiration in the exchange of ideas, basked in a relaxed and lively atmosphere.

Q1：更关心孩子成长，还是自我的更新迭代？

Amanda
（1）注重孩子的成长包括陪伴孩子，孩子并不在乎妈妈的提升，对妈妈的提升没有概念，他只在乎有没有人陪，包括生病、做游戏等时刻。

Q1: Prioritize children's growth or self-development?

Amanda
(1) Pay attention to the growth of children, including giving them company. Children do not care about their mother's improvement and have no concept of their mother's improvement. They only care about having someone there to be with them, including at moments of illness, playing games, etc.

（2）孩子的成长会给家庭带来很多的快乐和幸福的时刻。

（3）在孩子眼里，爸爸妈妈永远都是最棒的。而父母更加注重孩子的成长，孩子变得更优秀，也是家长的骄傲。

（4）龙生龙，凤生凤，老鼠的儿子会打洞。老鼠妈妈再怎么提升也是老鼠，不如提升老鼠宝宝，跟猫做朋友，得到生命的延伸。

Freya

孩子的成长是不可逆的，我们关注孩子的成长是为了给孩子足够多的安全感，有了这些安全感孩子才能有足够强大的内心去应对世界的不确定性和突发情况。

Jennie

（1）孩子是父母的生活中的一部分，而父母是小孩子的全部。父母是孩子的第一位老师，是最先影响孩子行为习惯、语言、性格的人。关注孩子的成长，把积极向上、乐观豁达和正能量传递给孩子。

（2）关注孩子成长的同时，不意味着

(2) The growth of children can bring a lot of joy and pleasant moments to the family.

(3) In the eyes of children, parents are always the best. Paying more attention to children's growth and helping them become a better version of themselves is also the pride of parents.

(4) Parents have a significant impact on their children's lives. No matter how much a mouse mother can improve, it is still a mouse. It is better to improve the mouse baby, and help the mouse baby make friends with cats, and get an extension of life.

Freya

The growth of children is irreversible. By focusing on their growth, we give them enough sense of security. With these feelings of security, children can have ample inner strength to cope with the uncertainty and unexpected situations in the world.

Jennie

(1) Children are a part of their parents' lives, and parents consists of the whole of their children. Parents are the first teachers of their children, and they are the first ones to influence their children's behavior, language, and personality. We should pay attention to children's growth and pass on positive, optimistic, and open-minded energy to them.

(2) Focusing on children's growth

忽略自身的成长和发展。父母要和孩子一起成长，共同进步。

（3）关注孩子茁壮成长，让他们拥有健康体魄、成熟心智、正确的价值观。一个积极向上、孝顺、懂得感恩的孩子足以温暖我们的下半生。

Heather

父母的世界观、人生观、价值观都对孩子有着决定性的影响。孩子是天生的模仿者，父母又是孩子最亲密、接触最多、对孩子最重要的人，所以应该与孩子共同成长。当父母教导孩子什么应该做、什么不应该做的时候，如果自己都做不到，经常玩手机，又如何让孩子相信父母说的"小孩子不应该玩电子产品"呢？

Jane

（1）榜样的力量是无穷的，龙生龙，凤生凤，老鼠的儿子会打洞。

（2）关心孩子的成长，不是简单计算陪伴的时间长短，而是要有效陪伴。

（3）孩子的潜力是无限的，而父母的能力和格局是有限的，单纯以自己视角的去关心只会束缚孩子。

does not mean neglecting our own growth and development. Parents should grow and progress together with their children.

(3) Pay attention to children's growth means helping them possess a healthy physique, a mature mind, and correct values. A positive, filial, and grateful child can warm us for the rest of our life.

Heather

Parents' worldview, outlook on life, and values have a decisive impact on their children. Children are natural imitators, and parents are children's closest, most connected, and most important people. Therefore, parents should grow together with their children. When parents teach their children what they should do and what they should not do, for instance, how can they make their children believe that "children should not play with electronic products" if parents cannot do it themselves and often play with their phones?

Jane

(1) The power of setting an example is infinite. Parents have a significant impact on their children's lives.

(2) Caring about children's growth is not simply a matter of the length of time spent with them, but a matter of quality time spent with them.

(3) The potential of children is unlimited while the ability and perspectives of parents are limited. Caring for their children only from their

（4）关心自己的成长不等于不关心孩子，而是要以更高效的方式给孩子的成长加杠杆。

Q2：寻找另一半，同频还是互补？

Jenna
两个志趣相投的人生活在一起，能减少很多不必要的摩擦，更容易营造良好的家庭氛围，有利于婚姻的稳定。选择另一半的时候，我会优先选择同频的。

Heather
同频的意思是两个人思想、意识、行为等方面协同统一，有共同的目标，一致的价值观，在情感上容易有共鸣。不管是伴侣还是朋友，同频的人更能理解对方的

own points of view can cast a burden on children.

(4) Caring about one's own growth is not the same as not caring about one's children, but rather a more efficient way to add leverage to children's growth.

Q2: Similar or complementary, what's the best partner?

Jenna
Two like-minded people living together can reduce a lot of unnecessary friction and is easier to create a good family atmosphere, which is conducive to the stability of marriage. When looking for the other half, I prefer people who are similar to me.

Heather
The meaning of like-mindedness is that two people are synergistically unified in their thoughts, consciousness, behavior, and other aspects, share common goals

情绪需求，欣赏和包容不同。

Jane

（1）客观上，物理学早就告诉我们，同频才能共振。在感情和婚姻中，同频就是能提升幸福指数，达到1+1＞2的效果。

（2）同频不是指完全一致，是同理和趋同，这种"同"能减少感情中的内耗，更容易的达到共同目标。

（3）同频的"同"，指共同话题。俗话说，话不投机半句多，"有的聊"常常是相处中最基本又最难得的。

（4）还有一个"同"，是共同的生活态度和处世哲学，感情一旦发展到婚姻，就是几十年的事，不同频的人一开始能碰撞出火花，后面就可能会爆炸。

（5）俗话说，平平淡淡才是真，感情最舒服的状态就是"你说的，我都懂"。

and values, and easily resonate with each other emotionally. Whether partners or friends, like-minded people are better able to understand the emotional needs of each other and appreciate and tolerate differences.

Jane

(1) Objectively speaking, physics has long taught us that resonance is only possible with the same frequency. In terms of relationship and marriage, like-mindedness can enhance the happiness index and achieve the effect where one plus one equals more than two.

(2) Like-mindedness does not mean being completely the same, but rather same reasoning and convergence. This similarity can reduce the internal friction in an relationship, contributing to the realization of common goals.

(3) One important aspect about like-mindedness is to have common topics. As the saying goes, half a sentence is too much for people with no shared interests. Having something to talk about is the most basic but also a difficult thing in a relationship.

(4) Another aspect about like-mindedness is to share a common life attitude and life philosophy. Once you get into marriage, it is a decades-long matter. Two people that are vastly different may have sparks of love at the beginning which turn into an explosion in the end.

(5) As the saying goes, being plain and simple is true happiness. The most

Joanna

择偶，我认为还是找"互补"型的。就以我自身为例，我和我先生，一个性格内敛，一个性格外向，大家觉得我们相处得怎么样？我们觉得相处得很开心。两个人能在一起，首先是因为对方身上有你没有的一面吸引着你，你才会有想要了解的欲望。

Amanda

（1）找互补的人，可以拓展彼此的能力，得到延展。

（2）有助于提升彼此的价值，共同奔赴，实现目标。

comfortable state of love is that the other person understands everything you say.

Joanna

I think it's better to find a "complementary" type of partner. Taking myself as an example, my husband is an extrovert and I am an introvert. Can we get along? Actually, we feel very happy together. The reason why you can get together with another person in the first place is that the person has a side that attracts you that you don't have, which is why you have the desire to get to know him or her.

Amanda

(1) Complementary partners can expand each other's capabilities and promote each other's self-development.

(2) Complementary partners can help each other improve themselves and

（3）同频的人容易放大缺点，虽然能互相理解，但是提升有限。

Fay

互补双方取长补短，各自发挥自己的优势，拓展生命的宽度，有利于双方的共同提升。1+1＞2，性格互补的双方包容力更强，能提供更多的新鲜感，使婚姻之路更为长久。

achieve their own goals.

(3) People of like-mindedness are prone to amplifying each other's shortcomings, and although they can understand each other, their improvement is limited.

Fay

Complementing each other's strengths and weaknesses, leveraging each other's strengths, and expanding the breadth of life is beneficial for mutual development of both parties. 1+1 ＞ 2. With complementary personalities, both parties have stronger tolerance, keeping the relationship fresh and exciting, and thus resulting in a long-lasting marriage.

3. 颁奖   Ⅲ. Award Session

最佳团体——双向奔赴队
Best Team—All-in-One Team

最佳着装:"窈窕淑女"奖
——Siki
Best Outfit: "My Fair Lady"
Award — Siki

最具人气:"智慧佳人"奖
——Jane
Most Popular: "Wisdom Beauty"
Award — Jane

Jane

特别感谢组织和赞助这次活动的同事，活动很难得，不仅增进了同事感情，也一定程度化解了大家的困惑和焦虑，相信大家也能借助这样的活动获得能量。不管工作还是生活，都能像 CEO 精心挑选的书——《幸福之路》一样，在幸福之路上，昂首阔步向前走。

Jane

Special thanks to the colleagues who organized and sponsored this event. It is a rare event that not only enhances the relationship among colleagues, but also to some extent resolves our confusion and anxiety. I believe that everyone can gain energy and momentum through this kind of events. Whether in work or life, just as indicated by the title of the book carefully selected by the CEO, *The Road to Happiness*, I hope that everyone can stride forward with head held high.

4. 幸福之路

活动的最后，CEO李燕飞女士分享了关于选择《幸福之路》的理由，在这个大放异彩的她时代，每一位职场女性都可以勇敢坚定地追随自己的职业理想，清楚地知道自己的优势，打破年龄界限，二十而立，三十而已，四十大有可为，敢于突破，不畏挑战，追寻成为更好的自己，绽放女性光芒！

摄影：李云龙
时间：2022年9月28日

IV. The Road to Happiness

At the end of the event, CEO Mrs. Fay Lee shared her reasons for choosing *The Road to Happiness*. In this era where women exhibit great talents in all aspects of life, every professional woman can bravely and firmly follow their career dreams, clearly know their strengths, and break the age limit. We all become independent at the age of twenty. Some of you are only in your thirties, and I believe that bright prospects still await even when we turn forty. We should dare to break through the boundaries, show no fear in the face of challenges, strive to become better versions of ourselves, and shine brightly and proudly as women!

Photographer: Chris Lee
Time: September 28, 2022

梦一样的 2022 年

2022: A Year Like a Dream

■ Tommy Chen

对我来说，2022 年是值得被铭记的一年，并不是因为这一年发生了多么让人愉快的事情，而是这一年极其特殊和梦幻。2023 年的篇章已经铺开，2022 年已成为过去时，但发生在这一年的事却令人久久不能忘却。这一年，我经历了最久的足不出户的规律的居家生活；同时，也经历了好几个第一次，第一次在现代化大都市感受到恐慌与焦虑、第一次与那个打了三年交道却不曾见面的"对手"零距离周旋……种种特殊的经历使我至今都在疑惑，过去的一年里自己的时空是不是发生了扭曲，那些曾发生在自己周围的人和事情究竟是不是一场梦。回首 2022 年，这一年里自己有过不甘心、焦虑和烦躁，也有过开心与成长，但更多的是一种心理上的释然。这一年让我明白了生活的好与坏是需要靠自己用心去把握的，很多时候要学会与自己及外界和解，只有学会接纳，脚下的路才会走得更宽。

For me, 2022 is a year to be remembered, not because many pleasant things happened during it, but because it was extremely uncommon, like an illusion. With the opening of the new chapters of 2023, the year 2022 has already become history, but what happened in that year will be long remembered. It was a year during which I experienced the longest time staying at home with a regular pattern of life. It was also a year that witnessed several records in my life: the first time that I had felt panic and anxiety in a modern metropolis, and the first time that I had engaged an "enemy" with zero distance whom I had fought with for three years but had never met…With all these special experiences, I wonder if my time and space was distorted in the past year and whether the people and things around me were just in a dream. Looking back on 2022, I have had a year of discontent, anxiety, and irritation, as

居家办公期间，不知是不是集中发生了太多事，自己的内心在经历了一波接一波的冲击后变得更加坦然；对于周围发生的人和事，无论好与坏，我从以前的毛躁，逐渐学会了接纳。闹情绪并不能解决问题，但有情绪一定会影响解决问题的思路。学会接受已经发生的事情，尽力掌握将要到来的生活，从过去中学习，在将来中成长。

6月，生活开始逐渐恢复正常。不知道是不是受到长期居家办公的影响，虽然身体已经踏出了家门，但心貌似还困在了之前居家的状态。本以为所有的生活已然开始回归本来的样子，但自己的状态显然没有及时调整过来。有时会分神，有时会莫名其妙地懈怠，明明主观上想去尽快完成事情，却莫名其妙地拖拉。自己曾多次反思过，究竟是什么原因导致自己的状态变差。其实所有的一切都可以归结于心态。心态不稳，即使能够做好的事情也会变得糟糕。生活就好比跑步，有的阶段体力充沛，有的阶段精神也会懈怠。但不论状态怎样，始终要靠自己去调整。漫漫人

well as happiness and growth, but more importantly, a mental release. I have been taught by what happened in that year that we need to distinguish the good from the bad in the life all by ourselves, and very often we must learn to reconcile with ourselves and the outside world; the road will become wider only if we learn to accept.

I don't know whether it was because too many things happened during the work-from-home period, but I became calmer and more confident after waves of impacts. Instead of being rash and irritable, I gradually learned to accept the people and things around me, no matter good or bad. Emotions do not solve problems, and being emotional will definitely affect our ability to solve problems. Learn to accept what has happened, try to be the master of the life that will come, learn from the past, and grow in the future.

Life began to return to normal in June. I wondered whether it was because I had been working from home for a long time, I seemed to be mentally stuck in the previous state though physically I had come out of my home. I thought our life had, as a whole, begun to return to what it originally looked like, but obviously I myself had not adjusted in time. Sometimes I get distracted, or slack off for no apparent reason. Sometimes I'm slowed down by inexplicable procrastination while I want to get things done as soon as possible. I have reflected

生路也像跑步一样，不知前方的路是什么样子，但只要意志坚定，把做好现在的事当作目标，时刻告诫自己不要拖拉，相信总有一天能够离梦想更近一步。

2022年已经成为过去，无论这一年自己开心与否，至少让我更加明白学会接纳是非常重要的。也许很多事情所产生的效果并不尽如人意，但经历即是学习，学习就能收获，无论是什么样的收获，学会接纳，从容面对，相信更美好的东西会不期而遇。

many times on the factors that have caused my worse performance. In fact, everything can be explained by mental attitude; if we are mentally unstable, we will end up with bad results even if we could have done it well. The daily life is like jogging, with stages when we are full of physical strength and stages when we slack off mentally. But no matter what stage we are in, it is always up to us to make adjustments. The long journey of life is also like jogging, we have no idea what the road ahead is like. But so long as we are strong-willed, set a goal of doing well on what we are working on at present, and always warn ourselves against procrastination, I believe that one day we can be one step closer to our dreams.

The year 2022 has become history. Whether I was happy or not in that year, at least it has taught me the importance of learning to accept. Perhaps many things has not delivered desirable results as we expected, but the experience itself is a process of learning, and if we keep learning, we are sure to gain something, no matter what kind of gains they will be. Learning to accept and facing adversity calmly, I believe that something better will come unexpectedly.

陈 浩
Tommy Chen

硕士毕业于英国伦敦玛丽女王大学，2020年9月加入施璐德。
Tommy graduated from Queen Mary University of London with a master's degree and joined CNOOD in September 2020.

立春到，万物兴

As Spring Sets In, Everything Prospers

■ Jerry Dai

《月令七十二候集解》里说："五行之气往者过来者续于此，而春木之气始至。"伴随着春天勃勃生机的回归，四季也由此拉开序幕。

历经寒冬的层层包裹与冰封，万物复苏。心动身暖，生命涌动出沸腾活力，注定又是一年人间烟火喧哗。天有寒来暑往，地有岁岁枯荣；在天则月圆月缺，在地则潮起潮落。立命于天地间，立春之日最需要立志。人生有大愿力，而后有大建树。渺小如我们，未必要有大作为，但不可没愿力。

It was written in *Commentaries on the Seventy-two Pentads*: "The *qi*, or vital energy, of the five elements of the past are continued here, and the *qi* of spring trees begin to arrive." With the return of spring's vibrant energy, the curtain has been raised for the four seasons.

After a freezing, icy winter, everything is revived. While we feel excited and warm, the surging vitality of life betokens another year of hustle and bustle. The heaven witnesses the alternation of seasons, while the earth the yearly withering and flourishing; the heaven sees the waxing and waning of the moon, while the earth the ebb and flow of the tide. As we live between the heaven and the earth, we must have ambition on the day of the Beginning of Spring. One can make great achievements only with great willpower. As insignificant as we are, we may not be able to do great things, but we must have willpower.

回望2022年，因工作结识了许多不一样的人，领略了祖国大江南北不一样的风景，体会了不一样的风土人情。犹记得出差广东成功参与项目审核和体系审核，在太仓驻厂顺利执行智利铜矿项目。即便同样的事情，遇到不同的搭档，也会擦出不同的火花。

读了《月亮与六便士》，价值观有了提升，书中月亮代表着远在天边的东西，代表着理想，六便士代表着面包，代表着生活。感谢作者带我领略了美丽的艺术世界，感谢作者带我穿越历史，向我传递人生价值观。

In the year 2022, I got to know many different people in my work, while I enjoyed different landscapes and experienced different local customs across our motherland. I still remember the successful participation in the project and system review in Guangdong and the successful execution of the Chilean copper mining project (Rajo Inca Project) in Taicang. Even for a same matter, there will be different sparkles when we encounter different partners.

My values have been refined since I read the book *The Moon and Sixpence,* in which the moon represents something far away in the sky and the ideal, while sixpence represents the bread and daily life. I would like to thank the author for a journey across the beautiful world of art and for guiding me through the human history and sharing life values with me.

自媒体时代，我结识了行者黎羽。他带我用行者的脚步丈量了祖国的大好河山，在行走中重新认识世界，在行走中重新认识自己。一个个温暖的趣事分享，一次次爱心的帮扶，都让我感叹生活的美好。

展望2023年，借用春节晚会上的几句话共勉："无问西东，向阳而生""椿萱并茂，感恩在心""不负雨露，花开有期"。我已经制定好了目标和计划，整装待发，续写新的篇章。

In the age of "we media," I got to know Li Yu, a hiker. He took me to measure the great rivers and mountains of our country with my footsteps and to know the world and myself again in hiking. The sharing of heart-warming episodes, together with the many cases of helping other people with loving care, moved me with the beauty of life.

Looking ahead to 2023, I would like to share with you a few words from the Spring Festival Gala: "Grow toward the sun no matter where you'll be going." "Be grateful that your parents are in good health." "There is a time for flowers to bloom, wasting not the morning dew." I have already set my goal and plan, ready to write a new chapter.

戴晓锋
Jerry Dai

2009年毕业于常州大学，后从事钢结构、船舶、海工等行业质量工作，2022年加入施璐德。

Jerry graduated from Changzhou University in 2009. He worked as quality engineer in the fields of steel structure, shipbuilding, and offshore facilities before he joined CNOOD in 2022.

春暖花会开

We Shall See Flowers in Bloom When It's Springtime

■ Jenna Hu

还记得 2020 年的时候写了一篇《不一样的春节》。那个春天，世界仿佛被按下了减速键、暂停键，车水马龙的道路变得空空荡荡，大街上熙熙攘攘的人群也消失了。时光荏苒，转眼三年过去了，这一年春回大地。

小时候写同学录，在"最喜欢的季节"那儿总喜欢写白色的冬天，就是下雪的冬天。因为下雪天很美，大地银装素裹，到处白茫茫一片，雪给世界披上了一层神秘的面纱。而且下雪天可以堆雪人、打雪仗，那都是孩提时的最爱，所以一到冬天就期盼下雪。如果天气预报说晚上会下雪，第二天早上醒来第一件事就是看窗户外面，要是看到雪积起来了，就会迅速穿好衣服冲出家门。童年是无忧无虑的，那时候不会考虑冷不冷、会不会生病，只关心好不好玩、开不开心。随着年龄慢慢增长，也可能是冬天越来越少下雪了，最

I still remember that I wrote an essay titled "An Unusual Spring Festival" in 2020. In that spring, the whole world suddenly slowed and came to a pause. The roads, which used to be crowded with vehicles, became totally empty, and the bustling crowd on the streets disappeared. Since then time has slipped by quickly. Three years have passed in a twinkling, and this year, the sweet spring has returned.

When I was a child, I always chose "white (i.e. snowy) winter" as my favorite season when writing in the school yearbooks. For me, the snowy days were extremely beautiful, with a vast expanse of whiteness covering the world in a mysterious veil. Besides, we could make snowmen and have snowball fights. Both were my favorites when I was a child, so I always looked forward to snowy days when it was winter. If the weather forecast said it would snow at night, the first thing I did after waking up the next morning was to

喜欢的季节变成了春天。我喜欢春天暖洋洋的温度，喜欢万物复苏，到处是一片生机勃勃的景象。

我的老家在横店，作为一个影视旅游小镇，最近三年游客大幅减少，景区外偌大的停车场里几乎没有车。疫情之前，每逢节假日，各个景点外面都车水马龙，经常堵车。就这样安静地度过了几个春节，2023年春节，游客们又回来了，过年期间经常能在社交平台刷到各个景点的盛况。景区外的餐厅人声鼎沸，小卖部的泡面都卖脱销了，开民宿的同学脸上笑开了花，说要让满房来得更猛烈一些。看新闻，全国各地的景点、商场也都人头攒动，大家又从家里走了出来，热闹的春节回来了。过年时最喜欢跟家人一起去商场买年货，看商场里来来往往的人们，听那喜庆热闹的音乐，觉得特别有年味，也能感受到即将到来的春天带给人们的希望与喜悦之情。

look out of the window. If the snow had heaped up, I would quickly put on my clothes and rush out of the door. Free from cares and worries, children thought only about whether it was fun; they were never bothered about the possibility of getting ill because it was too cold. As I gradually grow up, with less and less snowfalls in winter, spring has become my favorite season. I like the balmy weather in spring, with the revival of everything and all the vibrant scenes.

I was born in Hengdian, a small town famed for its film and television tourism. The town saw a significant decrease in the number of tourists during the past three years, with very few cars in the large parking lots outside the scenic area. Before the outbreak of the epidemic, there was always heavy traffic outside the tourist attractions, which often caused traffic jams. After several quiet Spring Festivals, tourists came back in the Spring Festival of 2023, and you could see on social media platforms what it was like at all the tourist attractions during the Spring Festival holiday. The restaurants outside the scenic area was bustling with tourists, while instant noodles were sold out in surrounding corner shops. My former classmates who run B&Bs were extremely glad, with big smiles on their faces, saying that "no vacancy" would come "in all its fury." Tourist attractions and shopping malls across the country, according to the news, were all seething with people, when everyone walked out of home again.The lively Spring Festival was back. I like going

春天是充满希望的，寒冬已过，暖春来临。正如旅游业经历了寒冬，疫情对我们行业也造成了冲击，所以大家对这崭新的一年充满了期盼。过完年回到公司，看到同事们都精神焕发、脸上洋溢着笑容。一年之计在于春，春天是播种的季节，大家纷纷摩拳擦掌，希望从春天开始就大干一场，跟过去的三年说再见，拥抱新的、美好的一年。

春天已到，期待花开。

to the malls with my family to do Spring Festival shopping. Seeing people coming and going in the malls and listening to the jubilant music, I felt strongly the festive atmosphere of the lunar New Year, as well as the hope and joy brought to us by the spring that was about to come.

Spring is a season full of hope. The chilly winter has passed, while the warm spring is coming. Just as the tourism industry has underwent a chilly winter, the epidemic has exerted an impact on the industry we are in. Therefore, we are now full of expectations for the coming year. When I came back to my office after the Spring Festival, I discovered that all my colleagues were in good spirits and beamed with smiles. As the saying goes, "A year's plan starts with spring." It is a season for sowing, and everyone is eager for action, hoping to go all out from spring, say goodbye to the past three years, and embrace a new, wonderful year.

It's springtime now; we are expecting flowers to bloom.

胡静航 Jenna Hu	信奉积极乐观、踏实努力的人生信条。 Jenna holds a creed of "Be active, optimistic, down-to-earth, and hard-working."

满怀希望方可所向披靡
Be Hopeful, Be Invincible

■ Hogan He

在喧嚣浮躁的时代，年轻人应该有一颗进取之心，开阔眼界、提升认知、不断进步。每个人的追求不同，使命也不同；但对于具体的每个人来说，不同的欲望只能在不同的台阶上得到满足。想要取得更大的成功，就要付出更多的努力。

当今社会，大多数人很难找准自己的定位。擅长做什么？适合做什么？该怎么做？多数人找第一份工作时，缺乏对自身的认识，缺少没有明确的职业规划，为生存而工作。我们很难有所突破，有所成就。这种情况下，多学习、多汲取新鲜事物和知识、多接触优秀的人尤为重要。这不仅帮助我们了解自己所擅长的领域以及真正感兴趣的事情，而且能让我们重新思考过去的思维方式和观念是不是错了。人改变的第一步，一定是思维方式和认知的转变。你和"头等舱"的距离，不仅仅是钱。

In noisy and impetuous times, young people ought to have the enterprising spirit, broaden their horizons, enhance their cognition and make continuous progress. People have different pursuits and different missions; but for each person, different desires can only be satisfied in different stages. You must put in more effort if you want to achieve greater success.

Today, most people find it hard to position themselves accurately in the society. What are they good at doing? What is the best thing that suits them to do and how should they do it? Most people lack both an understanding of themselves and a clear plan for career when looking for the first job. They work only for survival. It is difficult for us to make a breakthrough and achieve something. In this case, it is especially important to learn more, assimilate more fresh things and knowledge, and work with more talented people. This not only helps us

有人贩卖焦虑和危机，比如前段时间很火的网文，讲述了青年人的种种危机、贫富和生活质量的差距；也有人说岁月静好，最坏的结果不过是大器晚成。信息冗杂，有时会让人失去辨别能力。前者让人焦虑不堪，后者让人安逸平庸。事实上危机是存在的，保持危机感才能时刻清醒。但危机感和焦虑是两码事，后者只会让你陷入迷茫。你可以享受生活，但岁月静好不代表不需要加倍努力。既要在危机中找到动力，也要在生活中看到希望。

我们每个人生来就对未知的东西感到不安。我们追求稳定以及一切确定的东西，可人生就是充斥着各种不同的未知因素。大到人生选择，小到一件琐事，我们并不能掌控每一件事的确定性。我们能做的就是做好准备，迎接一切我们无法掌控的未知，要有逢山开路、遇水架桥的勇气。一定要弄清楚，我们目前

to understand what we are good at and what we are really interested in, but also enables us to rethink whether the past way of thinking and ideas were wrong. The first step in changing yourself is always a shift in your way of thinking and perception. The distance between you and the "first class" is not just about money.

Some people peddle their theory about anxiety and crisis. For example, an article went viral on the internet recently about the various crises of young people, the gap between the rich and the poor and the gap in the quality of life. Others say is that we are enjoying peaceful and good days and the worst result is just a late bloomer. The information is so cluttered that sometimes people lose their ability to discern. The former makes people anxious; the latter makes people idle and mediocre. In fact, crisis is always there, and one can remain sober-minded only by being aware of it. The awareness of crisis, however, is different from anxiety; the latter will lead you to nothing but confusion. You can enjoy life, but the "peaceful and good days" do not mean that you don't need to redouble your efforts. You must find motivation in crisis, and find hope in life.

We are all born with a sense of unease about the unknown. We seek stability and everything that is certain, but life is full of different unknowns. From life choices to the smallest things, we cannot control the certainty of every thing. What we can do is to be prepared to meet all the unknowns that we cannot control, with the courage to

所取得的成绩是平台造就的还是实力造就的。如果一定有什么是稳定的，那一定是你的能力，而不是你的职业。如果不去接触和学习新的东西，很难想象什么时候会被无情地淘汰。

人难以突破自己的舒适区，我们身处的环境很大程度上限制了我们的眼界和认知。人们喜欢跟朋友和身边的人比。这一点想必大家都有感受。但是，我们缺乏与外界比较。远在一线城市的同龄人年薪百万，你可能没有感觉；而能力不如你的朋友，如果月薪高你一些，心理就会不平衡。这也就是为什么很多人缺乏危机感的原因，他只看到了身边，却看不到外界的变化。

即便意识不到社会的发展趋势，也应该为现实的压力而奋斗。多数人需要背负房贷、车贷的压力，可薪水和欲望的落差太大，追求精致生活并不容易。工资也许会涨，但受地域、行业、岗位的限制，上涨的幅度不同。更重要的是，你未来的收入水平标志着你的能力范围。你能挣多少钱看的是能力和不可代替性，跟工作年限的关系并不大。讽刺的是，很多人有目标，实际行动却与目标背道而驰，需求与现实格格不入。

remove all the obstacles. Be sure to find out whether the achievements we have made so far are the result of the platform or the result of our own strength. If there has to be something stable, it must be your ability, not your career. If you do not go and learn something new, sooner or later you will be ruthlessly eliminated.

It is difficult for people to get out of their comfort zone, and the environment we are in limits our horizon and perception to a great extent. People like to compare themselves with their friends and those who are around them. I'm sure this is what we feel in common. However, we lack comparison with the outside world. You will probably be indifferent to someone of your age earning an annual salary of one million yuan in a first-tier city far away from you, but you will have a chip on your shoulder if one of your friends who is not as able as you earn a little more than you. This is why many people lack the awareness of crisis— they only see what is near them, but fail to see the changes in the outside world.

One should work hard under the pressure of reality even if he is not aware of the trends in the society. Most people have mortgages and car loans to pay, but with so big a gap between salary and desire that it is not easy to live a refined life. Wages may go up, but the rate of increase varies by region, industry and job. What is more important is the level of your future income, which indicates the range of your ability. The amount of money you can earn depends on your ability and irreplaceability

每登上一个台阶，都必须付出相应的成本。不仅面临巨大的竞争，还有自我意志的斗争。生活上这会占用你的业余时间，工作上会打破固有的思维方式和习惯。你可能很难接受朋友在歌舞升平时，自己却在忍受学习的寂寞；也很难接受高挑战的工作方式。但，这会形成一种习惯，成为你生活的一部分。这也就不难解释，为什么越优秀的人越努力。站在人生的终点来看，当我们回顾过去，是充满意义还是碌碌无为，都取决于我们现在每一个细微的选择，取决于选择不断学习和接受新的思想，还是吃喝玩乐、安于现状。

马太效应告诉我们：强者越强，弱者越弱。二八法则告诉我们：财富掌握在20%的人手里。社会贫富差距在扩大，阶层跨越变得越来越难。这是不可否认的社会现实。让人不禁怀念过去机会遍地的时代，你敢做就可能成功。

幸运的是，这个时代努力向上的通

and has little to do with the years of service. Ironically, many people do have their goals, but their actions run counter to the goals, that is to say, their needs are incompatible with the reality.

For every step up the ladder, there is a cost to be paid. Not only do you face great competition, but there is also a struggle of self-will. In your personal life, it will take up your spare time; in your work, it will break the old way of thinking and old habits. You will have a hard time accepting the loneliness of studying while your friends are singing and dancing; it will also be hard for you to accept the highly challenging way of working. But, it will form a habit and become a part of your life. It is not difficult to explain why better people work harder. When we look back before we die, whether we have lived a meaningful life or a vain and humdrum one depends on every small choice we are making now: to continuously learn and absorb new ideas, or just have fun and be content with the status quo.

The Matthew effect tells us that the strong will get stronger, and the weak will get weaker. The 80/20 principle tells us that wealth is in the hands of the richest twenty percent of people. The gap between the rich and the poor in society is widening, while it is becoming increasingly difficult to cross the lines between social strata. This is an undeniable social reality. It makes people feel nostalgic about the old days when opportunities were everywhere, and you could succeed if you dared.

Fortunately, in this era, channel for

道还是打开的，努力奋斗还有机会实现目标。想起清华寒门女孩的演讲："世界本不公平，努力是你唯一的路。"竞争不断加剧，很难想象我们老去的时候，子女是否还有机会实现阶层的跨越。很多人才的出现都是几代人共同努力的结果，为他们打好基础也是一种担当。更重要的是，在物质之外，人要追求自我价值的实现。马斯洛需求的五个层次中，最高层次就是自我实现。我们给社会乃至世界带来价值，才是人生最大的意义。

向上的通道总是痛苦的，而保持现状则是舒适的。当然这一切没有对与错，它只是一种选择和价值观判断。世界上只有一种英雄主义，那就是看清生活的真相之后，依然热爱生活！未来可期，满怀希望方可所向披靡！

upward mobility is still open, and there is still a chance to achieve your goal by working hard. I recall the speech of a girl from Tsinghua University, who comes from a humble family: "Of course the world is not fair, and your only way is to work hard." With the increasingly fierce competition, it is hard to imagine whether our children will still have a chance to cross the lines of strata when we grow old. The emergence of talents, in many cases, is the result of the joint efforts of several generations, and it is a kind of commitment to lay a good foundation for them. More importantly, people should pursue the realization of self-value beyond material conditions. Self-actualization is at the highest level in Maslow's hierarchy of needs. The greatest meaning of our life lies in the value we give to the society and the world.

The upward channel is always painful, while it is comfortable to maintain the status quo. Of course there is no right or wrong in all this; it is just a choice and a judgment about values. There is only one heroism in the world: to see the world as it is and to love it. The future is promising; we can be invincible only if we are full of hope!

何 禹
Hogan He

普通且热爱生活，爱好投资理财、打羽毛球。

Fond of financial investment and playing badminton, Hogan is an ordinary person who loves life.

金山城市沙滩

Jinshan City Beach

■ Cici Kang

金山城市沙滩是一个位于金山的沿海沙滩。沙滩上的景色无比美丽，有一望无际的大海，也有泛着金光的沙地。

在没有尽头的海里游泳无疑是夏日里最快乐的事。夏日早晨，海滩上的人可真不少，这些人中很多是小朋友，他们有的在岸上玩沙子，有的正套着游泳圈在海里戏水。浪花拍打着孩子，洋溢着一片欢声笑语。

夏日的中午，火辣辣的太阳尽情地照耀着沙滩和大海，大海上更加波光粼粼。在黄丝带一样的沙滩上散步，是一种再美好不过的感觉了。走在沙滩上，沙子异常烫脚，这温度足以煎熟一个鸡蛋了。

傍晚时分，红红的太阳照红了天，也

Jinshan City Beach is a coastal beach located in Jinshan District, Shanghai. The beach is unbelievably beautiful, with a vast expanse of sea as well as golden sands.

It is undoubtedly the most joyful thing in summer to swim in the endless sea. On summer mornings, there are quite a number of people on the beach, many of whom are kids. Some of the kids are playing with the sand while others are splashing around in the sea with swimming rings. The waves lap gently at them, and the beach is brimming with laughter.

At noon in the summer, the scorching sun shines on the beach and the sea, and the sea shimmers. Walking on the yellow ribbon-like beach is a most fantastic experience. When you walk on the beach, you can feel the burning sand which is hot enough to fry an egg.

At dusk, the sky and the sea turn

映红了海，天上偶尔有一两只海鸟飞过，海上偶尔有一两条小船飘过。日落时，沙地的温度已经凉了下来，在柔软的沙地里走着，身后留下一个个小脚印。随手捧起一把沙子，这么细腻，这么光滑。我想，海滩上的"星星"应该比太空中的星星还多吧。

金山城市沙滩可真好玩，既能在海里戏水，也能在沙滩上漫步，欢迎你们来玩！

crimson under the red sun, with one or two seabirds flying across the sky and one or two small boats floating over the sea. At sunset when the sand has cooled down, people walk in the soft sand and leave small footprints behind. If you pick up a handful of sands, you will find them so delicate and so smooth. I guess there are more "stars" on the beach than there are in the space.

Jinshan City Beach is really an interesting place where you can play in the sea and take a stroll along the beach. Welcome to it and have fun!

康钰轩
Cici Kang

施璐德二代，风一样的女子，明媚而温柔，坚定而执着。柔和的时候温馨拂面，如雨后清风；狂奔的时候自由自在，如脱缰野马。

As the child of a CNOODer, Cici is a girl like the wind; she is bright, sweet, firm, and persistent. When she is mild, she is like a pleasant, gentle breeze after the rain that kisses your face; when she is running about madly, she is as free as a wild horse.

一直在路上
——记录忙碌又平凡的一年

Always on the Road
— My record of a busy, ordinary year

■ David Lee

2022年这一年发生了太多大事件，如汤加海底火山喷发、俄乌军事冲突爆发、极端天气频繁出现、美元持续加息、欧洲能源危机爆发等。这些事件犹如发生在昨日，历历在目，让人不禁感叹时光飞逝。这一年对每个人来说都是不平凡的一年，一半核酸，一半心酸。疫情虽然限制了人们的步伐，但没有控制住我们对生活和工作的热爱。对我来说，这一年我一直在路上。

The year 2022 witnessed too many big events: the underwater volcanic eruption in Tonga, the outbreak of Russia-Ukraine conflict, the frequent occurrence of extreme weather, the continued interest rate hike of the US dollar, and the outbreak of Europe's energy crisis. They leap up vividly before the eyes as if they happened yesterday, and one can't help but sigh at how time flies. It has been an extraordinary year for everyone, partly because of PCR testing and partly because of sorrow. The epidemic limited people's pace, but did not suppress our love for life and work. For me, I was on the road throughout the whole year.

2022 年 1—5 月　秦皇岛

2022 年初在中铁山桥，摩洛哥钢箱

January–May 2022　Qinhuangdao

In early 2022 when I worked with

梁项目进入收尾阶段，我的主要工作是确保项目按期完工、审核项目资料和安排钢箱梁装船发运。按期完工是核心目标，而该目标的实现需要多方配合。我通过了解各相关方的最终需求和期望，进行高效沟通和协调，完成项目制定的目标和计划。在沟通中发现没有解决的问题，及时寻求项目团队的帮助。最终在整个项目团队的配合下，工厂成功完成交付任务。项目资料的审核工作不仅需要大量的时间和精力，更需要我对项目要求和工厂生产过程有充分了解。通过每天到现场了解生产状态，极大地提高了审核资料过程中对每个钢箱梁几千条焊缝的逻辑关系和每处信息追溯的正确性的判断能力。产品越复杂，对判断能力要求越高。产品装船发运前，在没有配载的情况下，我提前到码头实地了解情况，安排将该批次发运的产品提前转运至码头指定位置。在拿到具体配载后，规划出最短时间的装船方案（即最少的吊车翻箱次数和最少倒短调头次数）。通过不断积累经验和与各方的磨合，从第一批的 7 天缩短到第二批的 6 天再到第三批的 3 天，三批装船时间一次比一次短，为公司和客户节约了几十万元的成本。通过收尾工作，进一步锻炼了沟通协调能力，磨炼了记忆力、耐心，并丰富了复杂钢结构场地规划和装船经验。除了个人成长，团队的成长和经验总结对公司来说也是不可或缺的宝贵财富。

China Railway Shanhaiguan Bridge Group (CRSBG), the Morocco Steel Box Girders Project was in its concluding stage. My main tasks were to ensure the on-time completion of the project, review the documents and arrange the shipment of the steel box girders. On-time completion was the core goal, which required multi-party cooperation. To accomplish the goals and plans set for the project, I communicated and coordinated efficiently by understanding the ultimate needs and expectations of all parties involved. I sought help from the project team whenever I met with unsolved problems during the communication. Eventually, the plant successfully fulfilled the delivery tasks with the cooperation of the whole project team. The review of project materials required not only a lot of time and effort but also a full understanding of the project requirements and the production process. By visiting the production site every day, I kept myself informed of how things were going and greatly improved my judgement of the logical relationship among thousands of welded seams and the correctness of information traceability of each steel box girder when reviewing the materials. The more complex the product, the higher the requirement for my judgment. Before the shipment, I went to the wharf in advance in the absence of cargo, arranged to transfer that batch of products to the designated position in the wharf. After getting the

这中间有一个小插曲，由于秦皇岛对来秦人员隔离要求比较严苛，为不影响后续装船工作，项目完工后，我没有马上回上海，逃过了上海的静默管理，但与老婆的相见又晚了3个月，再回上海时已是2022年下半年。虽然无法切身感受静默造成的不便，但从很多渠道了解到上海人民在此期间的不易。其间除了工作和学习外，通过自学视频，我尝试做了一些平时没有机会做的菜品。洗菜时水流的"哗哗"声、切菜时刀板碰撞的"咚咚"声、油在锅里升温的"滋滋"声、菜入锅时的"噼啪"声和翻菜时锅铲发出的"珰珰"声，犹如一曲厨房交响乐，自己感觉进入

specific cargo, I worked out the loading plan with the shortest time (i.e., with the minimum shifting by container handling cranes and the minimum turning around in short-distance transport). Through continuous accumulation of experience and cooperation with all parties, the loading time became shorter for every batch, with seven days for the first batch, six days for the second, and three days for the third, saving hundreds of thousands of yuan for the company and our client. Through the closing work, I enhanced my communication and coordination skills, sharpened my memory, and cultivated my patience and perseverance, while enriching my experience of site planning and shipping for complex steel structures. I have realized that, in addition to personal growth, the growth and generalized experience of a team are also indispensable and valuable assets to the company.

At that time there was an interlude. Because the city of Qinhuangdao imposed very strict quarantine requirements for visitors, I did not return to Shanghai immediately after the completion of the project in order not to affect the subsequent work of shipment. As a result, I evaded the standstill orders in Shanghai, but I was unable to see my wife until three months later in the second half of 2022. Although I couldn't feel personally the inconvenience caused by the standstill orders, I learned from many sources how difficult it was for residents in Shanghai.

了心流的状态。满足味蕾的同时，我也获得了一丝成就感，很享受那段自己做饭时的慢时光。

2022 年 6 月　烟台

2022 年 6 月初，我回了一趟烟台老家看望亲人，跟老妈去了趟家附近的海边，让我回想起父母曾经经常带我赶海的快乐时光，抓螃蟹、堆城堡、捡海星海带、寻鹅卵石、看海鸥、听海浪声、环海骑行；刚好赶上老家最后一批樱桃上市，二姨带着我在市集上反复挑选，生怕选到不甜的坏果；90 多岁的姥姥，身体很健康，除了要大声跟她讲话外，交流无障碍，会用微信，平时偶尔打打视频电话，国家大事、时政要闻老人家都清楚；院子里的石榴树硕果累累，也刚好熟了，听说丁丁爱吃石榴，姥姥非要寄一大箱子，拦都拦不住。每次回老家，感觉海还是那片海，树还是那棵树，一直都没有变过，而我们成长了，亲人变老了。爱在烟台，不舍离家。

During this period, besides working and studying, by watching self-learning videos, I tried to make some dishes that I hadn't had the chance to make before. The various sounds in the cooking—the gurgle of running water when I washed the ingredients, the rat-tat of the kitchen knife and the chopping board clashing together, the sizzle of the oil heating up in the pan, the crackling when I put the ingredients into the pan and the clank of the spatula when I turned them—formed a "Symphony of the Kitchen." It seemed that I had been in the state of mental flow. While satisfying my taste buds, I also gained a sense of accomplishment and enjoyed the slow time of cooking by myself.

June 2022　Yantai

At the beginning of June 2022, I went back to my hometown in the city of Yantai, Shandong Province to visit my relatives. I went to the beach near home with my mother, reminding myself of the happy times when my parents used to take me to the beach to catch crabs, make sandcastles, collect starfish and kelp, look for pebbles, watch seagulls, listen to the sound of waves, and cycle around the sea. It was the time when local cherries were available on the market before they were out of season, and my second aunt took me to the market, picking the fruit repeatedly for fear of bad fruits that were not sweet. My grandmother, who was over 90 years old, was in very good health.

We didn't have any difficulty in talking with her, except that we must speak to her in loud voices. She used WeChat and occasionally made video calls, and was well informed with all the current affairs. The numerous fruits on the pomegranate tree in the courtyard were ripening, and my grandmother, knowing that Dingding liked eating pomegranates, insisted on sending a large box of them to us. Every time I go back home, I feel that the sea and the tree are still the same as they used to be, never changing, while we have grown up and our relatives have become old. With love for hometown, it is hard to leave it.

2022年6—10月　合肥和新疆

June–October 2022　Hefei and Xinjiang

享受了两周的"妈妈味"的饭菜后，摩洛哥钢箱梁管桩增补项目开工在即，我便马不停蹄地赶往合肥，开始新的征程。在项目执行过程中，我们遇到很多困难，比如隔板制作难度大、单节配套复杂、百年不遇的极端高温天气、疫情管控制约等，都是预期之外的不确定因素，对项目的进度造成了极大的挑战。为此我们与工厂进行大量的协调工作，针对较预期翻倍的隔板焊接工作量和制作难度，除了增加高水平焊接人员、打磨人员以及场地外，还要跟工厂确定最优制作工序，不断优化向监理方的报检流程，使项目顺利度过磨合期。该项目分两个场地进行：合肥场地负责钢管卷制、接长和隔板焊接，南通场地负责接长后的钢管总组、防腐和发运。为确保后端生产进度，我们跟工厂一起协调单节配套顺序，确保每天发运的单节配

After two weeks of enjoying "mommy-flavor" foods, I went non-stop to Hefei, Anhui Province to start new work as the Morocco Port Additional Piles Project was about to kick off. When executing the project, we met with many problems, including the difficulty in bulkhead manufacturing, the complexity of single-section combination, the once-in-a-century extreme high-temperature weather, and the epidemic control restrictions. These were all unexpected factors of uncertainty, posing great challenges to our schedule. Therefore, we did a lot of coordination with the plant, and considering the doubled welding workload and difficulty in the bulkhead manufacturing, we worked with the plant

套，保证南通环焊防腐场地的生产所需用量。为应对极端高温天气，我们不得不把工作时间从两班调整到夜班；为了应对缩短了的工作时间，我们成功跟客户争取到更长的工期，使项目最终满足客户安排的船期。其实，这个项目给我留下最深的印象就是奋斗在一线的人。在超40℃的车间里，哪怕走几步都会汗流浃背，而不同工序的工人、质检员和监理一直坚守在各自的工作岗位，即使衣服一直都是湿透的，依旧保质保量地完成工作。这种状态一直持续了3个多月，向可爱可敬的奋斗者们致敬。

to determine the optimal manufacturing process and continuously optimized the inspection process for the supervisors in addition to increasing highly skilled welders, grinders and sites, to ensure a smooth period of breaking in for the project. The project was carried out in two sites: the Hefei site was for steel pipe coiling, lengthening and bulkhead welding, while the Nantong site was for the general assembly of steel pipes after lengthening, corrosion prevention and shipment. To guarantee the back-end production schedule, we coordinated with the plant about the sequence of single-section combinations to ensure the daily shipment of single-section combinations to support the required amount of production at the Nantong site for ring welding and corrosion prevention. To cope with the extreme high-temperature weather, we had to adjust the working hours from two shifts to a night shift, and with the shortened working hours, we negotiated with the client and succeeded in extending the time limit of the project so that we managed to meet the shipping deadline set by the client. In fact, what impressed me the most about this project was the people working hard on the front line. In a workshop with a temperature of over 40 degrees Celsius, where one would soon be sweating all over after walking a little, workers, quality inspectors and supervisors of different procedures stuck to their posts. Even though their clothes were wet all the time, they finished their

7月底，为了弥补三个月不能相见的老婆，我忙里偷闲安排了新疆一周自驾行。我们从喀什出发先向南抵达塔什库尔干又折返向北到达伊犁。喀什的古城古巷、慕士塔格峰的彩虹、盘龙古道的曲折蜿蜒、独库公路起点的大峡谷和荒漠、巴音布鲁克的草原和山林、赛里木湖的天空之镜，串在一起，就是视觉天堂，令人震撼到语塞词穷。我会记得，那一年，我们越过白云悠远的高山，蹚过冰川融化的河流，穿过茫茫无际的草原，旅行的真谛大概就是带着灵魂去远行。

work with both quality and quantity ensured. Things went on like this for more than three months. Salute the lovely, respectable workers!

　　At the end of July, to make up to my wife for my absence of three months, I took some time out of my busy schedule for a one-week driving trip in Xinjiang. We started from Kaxgar, headed south to Taxkorgan, before turning north to Ili. The ancient town and alleys in Kaxgar, the rainbow seen from Muztagata, the twists and turns of the Panlong Ancient Road, the great canyon and wilderness at the starting point of Duzishan-Kuqa Highway, the grasslands and mountains in Bayan Bulak, together with Sayram Lake's "mirror of the sky," provided an awe-inspiring visual feast beyond description. This was a year that I would remember, a year when we crossed mountain ranges shrouded by drifting white clouds, waded through rivers with melting glacier, and went through vast, boundless grasslands. The true meaning of travel is probably to go on a long journey with your soul.

2022年11—12月　上海、苏州

　　10月底项目结束后，我回到阔别已久的上海办公室，过上了"两点一线"规律的生活，其间参与若干个不同体量的投标或报价，在报价中不断学习新的产品和知识，拜访新的供应商，了解供应商的产品、能力范围、主要市场、优势并与之建立关系。

November–December 2022 Shanghai and Suzhou

　　After the completion of the project at the end of October, I returned to the Shanghai office and began a regular life, during which I was involved in several bids or quotations of different volumes, continuously learning new products and knowledge, visiting new suppliers, getting information about their products,

又是一年除夕夜，听着窗外久违的鞭炮声，我在义乌写完这篇文章，感觉这一年转瞬即逝。这一年跟家人聚少离多，去过十几个城市，与很多人或擦肩而过或深入了解，每个地方每个人都在我的生命中留下痕迹，给我不同的成长感受。就像卡尔·萨根说过："在广袤的空间和无限的时间中，能与你共享同一颗行星和同一段时光，是我莫大的荣幸。"希望通过这一年的回顾和总结，为 2023 年重新出发做好更充分的准备；希望在新的一年里，自己的身体和心灵总有一个在路上，去经历更多的精彩。

capabilities, key markets and advantages, and establishing business relations with them.

It is New Year's Eve again. I'm finishing this essay in Yiwu, Zhejiang Province while listening to the long-lost sound of firecrackers outside the window. It seems to me that the year 2022 has passed very quickly, during which my family and I spent more time apart than together, and I visited a dozen cities where I just passed by or got to know many people, with each place and person leaving some traces in my life and impressing me with different feelings of growth. As Carl Sagan said, "In the vastness of space and the immensity of time, it is my joy to share a planet and an epoch with you." By reviewing and summarizing my life and work in the past year, I hope that I will be better prepared to restart in 2023, and that either my body or my mind will be on the road to experience more wonderful things.

李晓光
David Lee

1991年出生于山东烟台,热爱生活,喜欢旅行。2016年毕业于复旦大学材料系,并加入施璐德。珍惜与施璐德的缘分,希望与大家庭的每位成员共成长。

Born in Yantai, Shandong Province in 1991, David loves his life and travelling. In 2016, he graduated from the Department of Materials Science, Fudan University and joined CNOOD. He cherishes the destiny that connects him with CNOOD, hoping to grow together with every member of this big family.

随 想

Random Thoughts

■ Joanna Lee

随性聊一聊最近的琐碎事情吧。

1. 教育

2023年9月，小朋友要上幼儿园了，关于择校问题，全家展开了讨论，争论焦点是选私立园还是公立园。就我个人而言，我比较倾向私立园，想在自己能力范围内尽可能给小朋友提供良好的教育资源。

我一直觉得人类在某些方面的不平等来源于教育的不平等，而教育的不平等，又会反过来固化不同阶层的差距。循环往复，人与人之间的差距就会越来越大。这就是为什么中国的父母都拼命培养自己的小孩，宁可缩衣节食，也要投入大量的金钱精力到孩子的教育上。虽说条条大路通罗马，怎奈有的人本来就出生在罗马。

I would like to talk casually about trivial matters that happened recently.

I. Education

My kid will go to kindergarten in September 2023. The whole family discussed about choosing a kindergarten, and the choice between private and public kindergartens became the focus of the debate. Personally, I prefer a private one because I want to provide my kid with the best education that I can possibly offer.

I have always believed that the inequality in certain aspects of human beings results from the inequality in education, while the latter will in turn solidify the gaps between different social strata. The cycle repeats itself, and the gaps between different people become bigger and bigger. That's why Chinese parents always exert their utmost for the education of their children; they would tighten their belts just to put a large

在我的认知里，孩子的教育水平不是到了大学才拉开差距的，而是从中学、小学，甚至幼儿园开始。当我还只是从书本上接受新鲜事物的时候，别的孩子已经到博物馆去现场感受航空航天的魅力与奥秘。孩子从小接受的每一点教育都在塑造他的认知，也在拉大同龄人的差距。起点不一样，孩子的命运也会千差万别。在自己的能力范围内，为孩子的教育做储蓄投资，争取给他最好的，我想是每个父母奋斗的目标。

当然现在也有很多中国父母转变了教育思想，认为读万卷书不如行万里路。窃以为，眼界和学识是可以同步培养的。

amount of money and energy into their children's education. It's true that all roads lead to Rome; unfortunately, some people were born in Rome.

In my opinion, gaps in education are not widened when our children go to university, but when they are at secondary schools, elementary schools, or even kindergartens. While I could only learn new things from books, other children were already going to museums to experience the fascination and mystery of the aerospace. Every bit of education a child receives from a young age will shape his perceptions, which, at the same time, are widening the gaps between peers. With different starting points, children will later have very different lives. It is the goal of all parents, I think, to invest in the education of their children and try to give them the best.

Of course, many Chinese parents have now changed their ideas about education, who believe that it is better to travel ten thousand miles than to read ten thousand books, and it is possible to acquire knowledge and broaden one's horizons at the same time.

2. 老人

最近刷视频，看到一句让我内心五味杂陈的话："热闹只是暂时的，孤独才是常态，像是做了一场热闹的梦，一场用了360天才入睡的梦。"结了婚，生了娃，再加上疫情三年，回家的次数越来越少，总有无数个理由，为不能回家寻求内心的安慰。2023年，我们一家三口回我娘家过年。我呢，从小是跟爷爷奶奶生活在一起的，每次回去，都是爷爷骑三轮车到村口去接我们，这次却没有他的身影，回去才知道，他2022年底出了车祸，已经卧床有半个月。我很愧疚，每个星期都跟他们视频，咋就一点都没有察觉到呢？平常心细如丝的我这段时间竟如此愚钝，反而让76岁的老太太反过来安慰我们。我知道，他们不告诉我是怕我担心，担心我的身体还未恢复，不想我来回折腾。

"树欲静而风不止，子欲养而亲不待。"多回去看看老人吧，有些东西，失去了就没办法挽回。

II. Old People

I was browsing videos the other day when I came across the following words that left me with mixed feelings: "Hilarity is only temporary. Loneliness is the normal. It's like having a buzzing dream, one that takes 360 days to fall asleep." After getting married and having a baby, with the three years of epidemic, I went home less and less. There were always countless excuses for not being able to go home, which I could use in seeking self-consolation. In 2023, our family of three went back to my parents' home for the Spring Festival. I lived with my grandparents when I was a child, and every time we went back, my grandpa would ride a tricycle to pick us up at the village entrance. This time, however, there was no sign of him. It was when I arrived at my parents' home that I found out that he had been bedridden for half a month after a car accident at the end of 2022. I felt ashamed and guilty: how could I fail to notice such a thing as I had video calls with them every week? As a person with a meticulous mind, I looked so slow-witted at that moment. In fact, it was my 76-year-old grandma who tried to comfort us. I knew that they didn't tell me because they didn't want me to be worried and shuttle back and forth when I hadn't recovered yet.

"The tree would be still, but the wind would not stop; the son wishes to look after them, but his parents will not tarry." Go back more to see your parents and grandparents. There are certain things

这次春节忘记了拍全家福，明年补上，也就只有过年的时候，一家人才能团团圆圆。

which, once lost, can never be retrieved.

I forgot to take family photos during this Spring Festival. I'll make up for it the next year when we have family reunion again for the Spring Festival.

李 敏
Joanna Lee

2020 年 3 月正式加入施璐德，喜欢美食，旅游，拍照，坚持做好自我，求真务实。座右铭：路漫漫其修远兮，吾将上下而求索。

Joanna joined CNOOD in March 2020. She is fond of delicious food, traveling, and taking pictures, and insists on being herself and being pragmatic. Her motto: "The way ahead is long and has no ending; yet high and low I'll search with my will unbending."

随 笔

Some Short Notes

■ Roger Lee

"岁寒，然后知松柏之后凋也。"松柏之志不因环境之恶劣而改变初心，历经人生苦，方见从容心。经过这三年，我们要时刻告诫自己，不要悲观，亦不要盲目乐观，持中庸之道看待事物，用辩证的态度面对生活。

春节，灯火万家，鞭炮齐鸣。此时，家是最温馨的港湾。泡一壶清茶，烧二三小菜，酌丝丝温酒，美哉！乐哉矣！

行于尘世，无论遇到多少风雨，历经多少严寒，都要努力吸收阳光雨露。岁月更替，四季轮回，哪怕未赏春光，

"Only when the year grows cold do we see that the pine and cypress are the last to fade." The pine and cypress have the will never to change the original aspiration because of adverse circumstances. The heart's calmness can be seen only after experiencing the hardships of life. After these three years, we should always caution ourselves not to be pessimistic or blindly optimistic. Instead, we should stick to the "Doctrine of the Mean" when observing things, while facing our life with a dialectical attitude.

During the Spring Festival, the sound of firecrackers can be heard everywhere with a myriad of twinkling lights. At this time, home is the coziest harbor. Making a pot of tea, cooking two or three dishes, and taking a sip of warm wine—How pleasant! How happy!

Living in this mundane world, we must try hard to absorb sunshine and rain despite the storms and bitter cold we have

也莫道岁月晚。不念过往，不道蹉跎，不畏将来。

endured. Year in, year out, the seasons follow each other in rotation. Even if you missed the beautiful scenes of spring, do not say that it is too late. Never be obsessed with the past, regret the waste of time, or fear the future.

李 品　Roger Lee

2014年5月加入施璐德亚洲有限公司，毕业于华东师范大学。

Graduating from East China Normal University, Roger joined CNOOD in May 2014.

让成长一路荣光，为梦想不负芳华

May Our Path of Growth Be Full of Glory, and Seize the Days for Our Dreams

■ William Qiu

不知不觉，加入施璐德已经快三年了。三年时间，说长不长，说短不短，作为一名施璐德员工，我是幸运的。在公司这棵大树下，大家共同努力，这棵大树稳健成长。回首这几年，在百年未有之大变局下，全球形势复杂严峻，市场和供应链仍未恢复正常。

每个施璐德人都有两个家，一个是家庭，另一个是公司。在家庭中，我可以收获家人带来的温暖和感动；在公司中，我可以享受成就带来的充实和获得感。即便在成长的过程中，遇到的很多困惑或者挫折，其实都是成长路上的助燃剂，最重要的是这些经历往往证明着我在前进、在成长，激励我不断突破自己。

Before I notice it, it has been almost three years since I joined CNOOD. It's neither a long period of time nor a short one, and I am lucky to be a member of CNOOD. Under the big tree of the company, we work hard together, and the big tree has been growing steadily. Looking back on the past few years, we find the global situation complicated and severe while the markets and supply chains have not yet returned to normal with the unprecedented changes unseen in a century.

Every CNOODer has two homes, one is the family and the other is the company. In my family, I receive the touching warmth brought by my family members; in the company, I enjoy the fulfillment and sense of achievement. The perplexities and setbacks that I have encountered are in fact the fuel for my growth; most importantly, these

依稀记得刚接触阿尔及利亚项目投标时充满困惑。对于这类大型EPC项目我比较陌生，感觉无从下手，在部门领导的指导以及团队成员共同协作攻关下，我逐步顺手起来。受疫情影响，我们不能与客户面对面沟通，但项目团队不惧挑战，不畏难题，依旧收获了客户的信任以及合作伙伴的认可，这无疑增强了团队的项目管理经验和专业技能。什么是"不可能"？什么又是"可能"？用行动给出答案，成长的路上不会一帆风顺，放眼望去，向上攀爬的路总是布满荆棘。

欧阳修有诗云："羡子年少正得路，有如扶桑初日升。"愿每一个小小的我们，都不辜负初生太阳般的青春，有一分热，便发一分光。我们有的是活力：遇见深林，可以辟为平地；遇见旷野，可以栽种树木；遇见沙漠，可以开掘井泉。最好的年纪不应碌碌无为，更应埋头磨砺，在属于自己的时代和光阴里，为施璐德十年愿景大干一番。

experiences often prove that I'm moving forward and growing, and inspire me to push myself.

I still vaguely recall the perplexity I felt when I dealt with the Algerian project during its bidding process. Unfamiliar with this type of large EPC projects, I didn't know where to start with. Luckily, with the guidance of department directors and the cooperation of the team members, my work went on smoothly. Due to the impact of the epidemic, we were unable to communicate face to face with our client. Nevertheless, the project team was not afraid of the challenge and all the setbacks and eventually gained the trust of the client as well as the recognition of our partners, which undoubtedly enhanced the project management experience and professional skills of the team. What is "impossible"? And what is "possible"? The answer is given by action. The road of growth will not always be smooth; looking around, we will find that the path is always full of thorns when we climb up.

The following lines were written by Ouyang Xiu (1007-1072), a great poet, historian and statesman of the Song dynasty: "How I envy you, young and prosperous/like the sun rising beyond the East Sea." May every one of us, no matter how insignificant, cherish the youth like the rising sun and give out light if we have heat. We are full of vitality: when we meet a thick forest, we can make it a flat land; when we meet the wilderness, we can plant trees; when we meet the desert, we can dig a well spring. At the best age, we should not lead a vain and humdrum life but should do our best to sharp up, and in times that belong to us, make great contributions to the ten-year vision of CNOOD.

仇林恩
William Qiu

江苏南通人，"90后"。性格低调沉稳内敛，人生信条是独立进取。从事工程行业十年，热爱收集明信片、跑马拉松，博求万物之理，以尊闻而行知。

A member of the post-90s generation, William come from Nantong, Jiangsu Province. As a low-profile, steady and introverted person, he hold a creed of "Be independent, be enterprising." Having been in the engineering industry for ten years, he is fond of marathon and collecting postcards. While seeking extensively the Way of the universe, he respects what he hears and puts into practice what he has learned.

2023 年，再次出发
2023, It's Time to Start Over

■ Johnson Shen

"这是人们会说起的一年，这是人们说起就沉默的一年。"

偶尔读到德国诗人贝托尔特·布莱希特的这句诗，不禁思绪万千。回望过去一年，很多人似乎不再像以往一样感慨，这一年怎么这么快就过去了，与其说怀念2022年，似乎更盼望它早点过去。

过去一年，我们被巨大的不确定性包围。在2022年的年终总结中，很多人感叹，疫情这几年，好像没做什么，时间就过去了；也有人历数这一年的失败与失去……我们常常会对那些无力感印象深刻，却常常忽视：这一路，自己穿越了多少暴风骤雨，熬过了多少焦虑与迷茫，却依然还在路上。

"This is the year which people will talk about. This is the year people will be silent about."

I was lost in a myriad of thoughts when I came across the above lines written by the German poet Bertolt Brecht. When we review the past year, it seems that many people no longer sentimentalize, as they used to, about how fast the year has passed. Instead of missing the year 2022, they wish it had ended earlier.

During the past year, we were surrounded by great uncertainty. In their year-end reviews of 2022, many people lamented that they had done nothing while time elapsed during the epidemic; others enumerated the failures and losses in the year... We are often impressed by our powerlessness, but often ignore the fact that we are still on the road after the many storms we have braved as well as the enormous anxiety and confusion we have experienced along the journey.

这是奇怪的一年，经历了一段特别漫长的过程，回首看来，又觉得特别快。

慢，是因为你想了很多，反复不断的疫情让你有了过剩的思考；快，是因为你可做得太少，疫情反复，你无法腾出时间使劲撒欢。所以有人躺平，有人围炉煮茶，大家的步子都放慢了。

回首 2022 年，很多事情还历历在目，令人印象深刻。居家期间，我经常望向窗外，天空时而晴朗，时而有阴郁的云朵压城。或许一个人注定要穿越荒漠，才能来到新的绿洲，遇见久违的鸟语花香。生活或许已经让人明白，通向远方的路从不是平整的大理石铺成的，我们终要打起精神。

It has been a strange year. After a very long process, we now think it has also been very fast when we look back on it.

· It's slow because you think a lot: repeated outbreaks of the COVID-19 epidemic have made you think too much. It's fast because you can do too little and you cannot spare the time to enjoy life with abandon. As a result, some people slack off while others cook tea around the stove: we all have slowed down our pace.

Looking back on 2022, I find many things still vivid and impressive. During the work-from-home period, I often looked out of the window. Sometimes the sky was clear, and sometimes there were gloomy clouds pressing down on the city. Perhaps one is destined to cross the desert before coming to a new oasis with singing birds and fragrant flowers. Life may have made it clear that the road to the future is never paved with smooth-faced marble, and we must finally brace ourselves up.

6月，走出家门。在公司领导和同事的共同组织下，我们毅然决定迈出步伐，走出国门，拜访客户，沟通项目。我们深知每一个项目的成功落地都需要付出数十倍的努力，走出去，不只是关乎所向何处，更关乎信念，关乎勇气与激情。

米兰·昆德拉说过："往哪走，都是往前走。"人最害怕的不是走错，而是害怕时停滞不前，那才是真正的倒退。所以，当你站在十字路口感到迷茫的时候，化解迷茫的唯一办法就是——迈开腿，

In June, 2022, the work-from-home period was over. Under the joint organization of company leaders and colleagues, we determined to take the step to go abroad to visit our clients and communicate about projects. We know that the successful implementation of each project requires dozens of times of effort. When we talk about "going out," it's not only about where to go, but also about faith, courage and passion.

Milan Kundera said: "Forward is anywhere." What people are most afraid of is not to go the wrong way, but to stand still when in fear—that is the real backsliding. So, when you stand at the

155

走出那一步。因为，重要的是你始终都在前进。

2023年，仍旧是充满机遇和挑战的一年。国内经济预期会复苏，但是在国际关系上可能还会遇到一些阻碍。我相信我们仍会坚守初心，用更多的努力来争取更多的机会。

无论是地理空间意义上的出发，抑或是心灵的转变，对于2023年，我们寄托了很多。未来或许还有很多不确定，但我们始终继续向前走。"新"年，我们以饱满的情绪，增加生活的厚度与层次。让我们可以拥有富有厚度的一生，让我们从过去中走出来，抬起头，向前看。

crossroads and feel lost, the only way to resolve the confusion is to lift your foot and take that step. The reason is: the important thing is that you are always moving forward.

2023 will also be a year full of opportunities and challenges. The domestic economy is expected to recover, but we may still encounter some obstacles in international relations. I believe we will still stay true to our original aspiration and try harder for more opportunities.

Whether it is a departure in the geospatial sense or a transformation of the mind, we are counting on a lot for 2023. The future may still be uncertain, but we will always continue to move forward. In the "new" year, we shall increase the thickness and depth of our life with high spirits. By doing so, we can have a rich and meaningful life. Let's step out of the past, lift our heads up and look forward.

沈佳祺
Johnson Shen

所有的相遇，都是久别重逢。不知不觉在CNOOD已经十年多了。这样一个关怀他人、提升自我的集体，始终能让我充满正能量。走遍世界的角落，带着自由而无用的灵魂。

Every occasion of encounter is a reunion after a long separation. I have been working at CNOOD for more than ten years before I know it. Such a caring and self-promoting organization always fills me with positive energy. With a free and useless soul, I'm going across every corner of the world.

十年施璐德
A Decade with CNOOD

■ Andy Wei

2012年1月29日，我正式加入施璐德大家庭，或许称之为施璐德"小家庭"更加贴切，因为当时的施璐德就是一个温馨、团结、奋斗且充满激情和阳光的"小家庭"。2023年1月6日，我正式被公司颁发"十年忠诚奖"。

恍惚间，十年时间如弹指一挥，我们的大家长经常挂在嘴边的"四心"（爱心、上进心、自信心、平常心）以及"做好一件事情，便什么事情都能够拿得起放得下"等经常给我们分享的想法始终萦绕在耳边。依旧清晰地记得十年前第一次步入施璐德的样子，回首望去，还是感慨颇多。整体而言，在过去十年我的人生还是顺风顺水的，感恩生命中遇到的贵人们。

On January 29, 2012, I joined the big family of CNOOD, or, to be more accurate, the "small family" of CNOOD, because at that time CNOOD was indeed a warm, united and endeavoring "small family" full of passion and positive energy. On January 6, 2023, I received the "Ten-year Loyalty Award" from the company.

Ten years have passed in the twinkling of an eye, and the "four states of mind" (love, ambition, confidence, and tranquility) which our boss often talked about and the ideas shared by him such as "by doing one thing well, you can pick up anything and do it well" are always ringing in our ears. I remember vividly how I walked into the company for the first time ten years ago. When I look back, I'm filled with a myriad of emotions. All in all, my life has been smooth in the past ten years, for which I'm grateful to those who have greatly helped me.

在生活上，我完成了结婚生娃、读书安家的人生大事，物质水平也较十年前有了巨大的提升。十年前曾畅想过自己现在的样子，记不清当时是如何想象现在的自己，但是我觉得现在的生活状态比我想象中的最好的样子还要好。

在工作上，遇到过一些风雨，但是走过风雨就能见彩虹。过程虽有些波折，但结局总归是美好的。刚步入施璐德的时候，作为公司最年轻的员工，得到的资源和培养可以说是施璐德创立以来最好的之

As for my personal life, I have got married, had a baby, completed my studies and settled down, with significantly better living conditions compared with those of ten years ago. Ten years ago, I gave free rein to my imagination while thinking of what I would look like now. I can't remember how I imagined about myself at that time, but I believe that my present state of life is better than the best I ever imagined.

I have encountered setbacks in my work. However, I can see the rainbow if I survive the storm. Notwithstanding the twists and turns, things always end well. When I joined CNOOD as the youngest

一。因为公司当时处于创立之初，成员多为经验丰富的合伙人，只有极少数的新人，所以我才有众多的机会去接触不一样的事情和人，向各位老师学习经验，在此特别感谢引导教育我的老师们。在工作中，最值得高兴的事情就是：教导过我的老师们有时候让我必须解决某事或者与我协商某个重大决定，这都让我感受到实现自我的满足感。公司人才济济，我肯定不是最优秀的，但是我在那个时间点上是最合适的"解"。

总结一下这十年：第一年，是积累大量经验和提升能力的一年，接触各种商务条款、文件、单据、邮件等，再之后是国内现场项目管理的数年，然后是2019年去缅甸的一年，缅甸回国后是工作岗位和性质发生转变以及受疫情影响在上海时间最长的两年。但是不论怎么变，在公司需要我的时候，我会改变自己来适应公司。十年里，除了工作以外，印象深刻的还有公司的春游和团建，武夷山、云南、海南、巴厘岛等，现在疫情结束，生活恢复了正常，我们一切顺利，继续一边工作一边玩。

member in the company, the resources and training I got were among the best since CNOOD was founded. Because the company was in its infancy, with mostly experienced partners and very few newcomers, I had many opportunities to access different things and people and learn from the tutors. I'd like to express my gratitude to them for guiding me. The most rewarding thing about my job is that the tutors sometimes let me solve something or discuss with me about a major decision, which makes me feel the satisfaction of self-actualization. With so many talented people in the company, I'm sure I wasn't the best, but I was the right "solution" at that point of time.

To sum up the past decade: the first year was the year of gaining a lot of experience and improving my ability, when I dealt with all kinds of business terms, documents, bills, emails, etc.; then several years of on-site project management in China, and the year of working in Myanmar in 2019; coming back to China thereafter, I experienced the change of job position and the longest two years in Shanghai affected by the epidemic. No matter how big the changes are, I am always ready to change myself to fit the company when it needs me. What impressed me during the ten years, besides the work, included the company's spring outing and team building activities in Mount Wuyi, Yunnan, Hainan, Bali, etc. Now that the epidemic is over and life is back to normal, everything is going

最后寄语加入施璐德大家庭的新人们：衷心地希望能听到你们的十年忠诚奖获奖感言。

well, and we continue to work hard while having fun.

Finally, a few words to the newcomers in the CNOOD family: I sincerely hope to hear your acceptance speech for the "Ten-year Loyalty Award."

魏 坤
Andy Wei

在施璐德亚洲有限公司工作超十年老员工，新晋奶爸。爱国、爱党、爱群众、爱公司，爱家庭。

A veteran who has been working at CNOOD for more than ten years and a new dad, Andy loves the country, the Party, the people, the company and his family.

德意志列车
The German Trains

■ Mira Wei

春运结束后,我和朋友聊到国内高铁、动车都很准时,如果晚点也就几分钟的事情。然后,我们开始对德国铁路进行又一轮的吐槽。一提到德国,大家第一印象可能就是德国人严谨又守时。确实,德国城市内部的公交车、电车每个站都会有车辆到达时刻表,这些时间点大多数情况下都还是很准时的。但如果你要跨城市或者说跨州就要坐类似国内的动车、高铁的 ICE(Intercityexpress)、IC(Intercity)和 EC(Eurocity)。其中 ICE 速度是最快的,票价当然也最高。

在德国生活过的人看来,"德铁准时"就是个笑话。在德国,当人们提起火车时

When the Spring Festival travel rush ended, my friends and I talked about the high-speed trains in China and found them very punctual, with only several minutes' delay if unavoidable. Then we started another round of sneering comments on Deutsche Bahn (meaning "German Railway" in English, the railway system of Germany). When talking about Germany, people's first impression may be that Germans are scrupulous and punctual. In Germany, buses and trams in a city generally have arrival schedules at each stop, which are accurate in most cases. But if you want to travel between different cities or states, you'll have to take ICE (Intercityexpress), IC (Intercity), or EC (Eurocity), similar to the high-speed trains in China. Among them the ICE is the fastest with the highest fares.

"German railway on time" is merely a joke to people who have lived in Germany.

候，首先说的就是晚点。我朋友经常从斯图加特坐车去汉堡，深受其害。无论是短途还是长途，列车经常会出现各种原因的晚点，延迟时间从10分钟、20分钟到1小时不等，甚至取消。2017年，我从杜伊斯堡搬家到慕尼黑时搭乘的火车，先是没有具体原因就在科隆停留1小时，最后在慕尼黑的前一个城市，所有人下车，搭乘对面过来的车前往终点站慕尼黑。整个过程，列车晚点2个小时。晚点的原因是多方面的，德铁公司自己认为，基础设施和车辆供应不足以及工作人员的缺乏是主要的问题。此外也有一些外部影响因素，如暴风雨、火灾、罢工、电缆盗窃、事故以及自杀。

除了经常晚点，德铁也还有别的点需要吐槽。连年上涨的票价也让人叫苦不迭。与国内所有火车票价格稳定不同，德国的火车票越早买价格越便宜。如果是出发前临时买票，4小时以上的ICE票价有时候可能要上百欧元。例如，从慕尼黑到柏林，1月31日票价为95.9欧元起，2月28日却很便宜，为17.9欧元。乘坐德铁出行仿佛是一场充满不确定的冒险，不知道什么时候出发，更不知道什么时候能够到达。当然能够投诉和抱怨，但是得到的也只是工作人员"真的很抱歉，我们也暂时没有得到消息"等带微笑的回复。

When people talk about trains in Germany, the first thing they talk about is the delays. My friend, who often takes the train from Stuttgart to Hamburg, suffers a lot from it. Both short-distance and long-distance trains are often late for various reasons, and the times of delay vary from ten minutes, twenty minutes to one hour; the train might even be canceled. In 2017, I moved from Duisburg to Munich on a train. The train first stopped in Cologne for one hour without specific reason and finally stopped in a city prior to Munich, where all the passengers were asked to get off and took the train coming from the opposite direction to the destination. The train was late by two hours in the end. The reasons for the delays were manifold, with Deutsche Bahn itself citing a lack of infrastructure, vehicle availability and a lack of staff as the main problems. There are also external influences such as storms, fires, strikes, cable theft, accidents and suicides.

Besides frequent delays, there are other reasons for us to satirize Deutsche Bahn. Rising fares year after year have caused discontent among the people. Unlike the stable train ticket prices in China, German train tickets are cheaper the earlier you buy them. If you buy the ticket at the last moment before departure, an ICE ticket for a ride over four hours sometimes costs more than a hundred euros. For example, if you travel from Munich to Berlin, the ticket price starts at 95.9 euros on January 31, but is

当然，德铁晚点后，乘客有权要求索赔。晚点超过 60 分钟，可以获赔票价的 25%；超过 120 分钟，获赔票价的 50%。

和国内坐车最大的不同是，火车站谁都能进入，不需要刷身份证。当然也没有安检流程，你只用找到自己列车所在的站台，上车就行了。火车票上也是没有固定座位号的，除非在买票的时候多加几欧提前预订座位。座位上方有个小电子屏显示这个位置是否被预订，或者显示在某一站到某一站之间被预订。另外，小型犬和小型宠物是允许免费携带的。如果是大型犬，需要支付票价的一半，相当于儿童票的价格。陪伴犬旅行一直是免费的。

much cheaper at 17.9 euros on February 28. Traveling by Deutsche Bahn is like an adventure full of uncertainty; you never know when you'll leave or when you'll arrive. Of course you can lodge complaints, but all you get is a smile from the staff saying, "I'm really sorry, but we haven't got any news yet" and so on.

Of course, passengers have the right to claim for compensation if the train is late. If the train is late for more than 60 minutes, you can claim 25% of the fare; if it is late for more than 120 minutes, you can claim 50% of the fare.

The biggest difference between German and Chinese railways is that everyone is allowed to enter any train station without checking their ID cards in German. In addition, there is no security check process. All you have to do is to find the platform where your train will stop at and get on the train. There is no fixed seat number on the train ticket, unless you spend a few extra euros to reserve a seat in advance when buying the ticket. There is a small electronic screen above each seat that shows whether the seat is reserved or not, or whether it is reserved between certain stations. Small dogs and pets are allowed to travel free of charge, and half of the fare should be paid for a large-size dog, equivalent to the price of a child ticket. Companion dogs are always free of charge when travelling by train.

魏媛媛
Mira Wei

湖北仙桃人，生活在上海。

Mira comes from Xiantao, Hubei Province, and now lives in Shanghai.

迎接 2023 年

Welcome to 2023

■ Amanda Wu

此刻坐在办公桌前，打开电脑，往事不断在脑海里浮现，平凡的工作和生活有很多精彩的瞬间，其间有同事和领导的关心，有家人的陪伴，顺利度过 2022 年，满怀期待迎接 2023 年。

和往常一样，我们长宁小分队经常蹭老虎的车一起回家，让这个冬天不再寒冷。在办公室讨论的大多是某个具体的项目和项目机会，回家的路上我们畅所欲言。老虎一直鼓励我们，如何当好一个项目经理，需要具备哪些能力，同客户开视频会议注意哪些细节等，我们倍受感动。

At this moment as I sit at the desk and turn on my computer, images of the past events flash through my mind. I have experienced a lot of wonderful moments, with the loving care of my colleagues and bosses as well as the company of my family. Now having getting through the year 2022, I'm looking forward to the year 2023 with great expectations.

As usual, Tiger often gave a lift to our Changning team in his car to go home together, making this winter no longer cold. Most of the time when we were in office, we would be discussing a specific project or potential opportunities for a project, but on our way home we would talk freely about anything. I was greatly moved by Tiger, who kept encouraging us and shared his ideas about how to be a good project manager, what capabilities we needed, and what details we should pay attention to when having video conferences with our clients.

任何不常见的产品，小分队中最年长也是最年轻的前辈丁总，总有办法找到靠谱的供应商，用他的话说"找到这个厂家，可以睡个好觉"。

Charles是公司金牌主持人，能胜任各场景，从重要的年度大会到日常欢乐的生日派对，都拿捏得很好，而且可以中英双语自由切换。

2022年，我们小分队忙得热火朝天。在完成工作的情况下，有当小区志愿者的，有在家练厨艺的，有带娃带到感觉世界末日来临。大家在小分队微信群里分享生活中的点点滴滴，互相关心。

最近半年，我有机会参与业务组的很多项目，不论是Fay姐直接联系我，还是通过Andy转发，都会有一句话："有任何问题都可以来问我。"这句话伴随着每一个项目机会和询盘，鼓励我更加仔细认真地对待每一个询盘。

过去一年执行过项目，发掘过项目机会，2023年我将继续努力前行，希望这些机会可以开出美丽的花朵，结下丰硕的果实。

Mr. Ding, the eldest and yet youngest senior member in the team, always had a way to find a reliable supplier for any uncommon product. As he said, "Now that I've found this manufacturer, I can have a good sleep."

Charles is the golden MC of our company and can handle all kinds of scenes. He always did a wonderful job of hosting important annual meetings as well as happy birthday parties. In addition, he can switch between Chinese and English freely.

In 2022, all the members of our team were extremely busy. In addition to our work, some became community volunteers, some practiced cooking skills at home, while others were knackered when looking after their children. We shared these moments of our life in our WeChat group and expressed our care for each other.

During the past six months, I have had the opportunity to participate in many business projects. Fay would contact me directly or forward the information through Andy, and there were always the words "feel free to ask me about anything," which went with every project opportunity and every inquiry, encouraging me to deal with every inquiry more carefully and seriously.

I have executed projects and explored project opportunities in the past year, and will keep working hard in 2023, in the hope that these opportunities will blossom beautifully and bear rich fruit.

附：宝宝闲话

场景一

在公园里，宝宝想让我抱他，在他多次请求下我便答应了，可没走几分钟，我感觉宝宝越来越沉，越来越往下坠……

我：妈妈搞不动了。
宝宝：搞不动是什么意思？

我：搞不动就是抱不动的意思。

宝宝：是完蛋的意思。

场景二

宝宝最近喜欢看绘本《波西和皮普》，讲的是是一只名叫波西的老鼠和一只名叫皮普的小兔子在各种场景发生的故事。晚上关灯睡觉的时候，宝宝经常嚎啕大哭，要求再看会《波西和皮普》。他是真的想看还是不想关灯睡觉？春节期间，我带宝宝去投喂小动物，恰好小兔子和老鼠离得很近，笼子挨着。

我：可可，你在喂什么小动物？

宝宝：我在喂波西和皮普。

宝宝喜欢的绘本极少极少，他通常把书拿来当玩具，扔地下踩，拿手上撕，塞

Keke's Prattle

Scene One

In the park, Keke wants me to hold him in the arms. With his repeated requests, I agreed. But I did not walk a few minutes before I felt that the kid was getting heavier and heavier.

I: Mom is out of strength.
Keke: What do you mean you are out of strength?

I: It means I can't hold you any more.

Keke: It means you're toast.

Scene Two

Recently Keke is fond of the picture books *Pip and Posy*. The series is about stories of a mouse named Posy and a rabbit named Pip on various occasions. When the lights are turned off at night, he often cries out and asks to read a little more of *Pip and Posy*. Does he really want to read them, or does he simply not want to go to bed? During the Spring Festival, I took him to feed little animals, and it happened that the rabbits and the mice were very close to each other, living in neighboring cages.

Me: Keke, what little animals are you feeding?

Keke: I'm feeding Posy and Pip.

There are very few picture books that Keke likes reading; he usually treats them

嘴里啃，但《波西和皮普》至今保存完好，这可能是真的喜欢吧！

场景三

宝宝喜欢吃零食，尤其喜欢奶酪棒、草莓、葡萄、酸奶，类似这些的健康的奶制品和水果，我们一般都会满足他。而有些不适合宝宝吃的，比如薯片，宝宝最多拿一片尝尝，他自己也知道爸妈不给他多吃。

宝宝吃奶酪棒或者草莓、葡萄的时候，我们故意试探他，让宝宝分享给我们。

as toys, throws them on the ground and steps on them, tears them by hands and even chews them in his mouth. However, the *Pip and Posy* series has so far been kept in good condition. So perhaps he really likes them!

Scene Three

Keke likes eating snacks, especially cheese sticks, strawberries, grapes and yogurt. For these healthy dairy products and fruits, we usually satisfy him. And for those snacks unsuitable for little kids, such as potato chips, he will take a piece at most, knowing that we won't allow him to eat too much of them.

When Keke is eating cheese sticks, strawberries or grapes, we would deliberately test him and ask him to share the food with us.

我：可可，你在吃什么好吃的？

宝宝：草莓。

我：拿个给妈妈吃吧？

宝宝：妈妈吃了牙痛、肚子痛，不能吃。

我：妈妈吃了牙痛，你吃不牙痛吗？

宝宝：可可吃了牙不痛，全部都吃完。

宝宝看到柜子上有盒薯片，推来椅子踮起脚站上面。终于拿到薯片了，他估摸着我们可能不给他拆。

宝宝：这是什么？
爸爸：我也不知道。
宝宝：可可知道，这是薯片！大家一起分享吧！
爸爸：薯片不适合你吃，要不吃点别的吧？
宝宝：吃一点没关系的。

于是，无底线的爸爸便同意了。

生活还在继续，这个小伙子在他的成长轨道上前行，希望我们和平相处，多一些母慈子孝的场景。

I: Keke, what are you eating? They look yummy!

Keke: Strawberries.

I: Give one to mom, OK?

Keke: No. You'll have a toothache and a stomachache if you eat it.

I: I will have a toothache when I eat it. Will you have a toothache when you eat it?

Keke: No, I won't. I will eat them up.

Keke saw a packet of potato chips on the cabinet. He then managed to move a chair near the cabinet, climbed onto the chair and stood on tiptoe to reach for the packet. Finally getting it, he figured we might not open the packet for him.

Keke: What's this?
Dad: I don't know.
Keke: But I know. It's potato chips! Let's share them!
Dad: Chips are not for you. What about something else?
Keke: It's okay to eat just a little.

Then, his dad with no bottom line agreed.

Life goes on, while this young man is moving forward in his way of growth. I hope that we live together in peace, with more scenes of mutual affections.

邬 成
Amanda Wu

毕业于上海大学材料工程专业，2016 年加入 CNOOD。

Amanda graduated from Shanghai University majoring in materials engineering and joined CNOOD in 2016.

幸福在哪里
Where Is Happiness

■ Ada Wang

匆匆忙忙，熙熙攘攘，
我们都在追求幸福，
可幸福好像在遥远的天边，又在遥远的未来！
幸福，在哪里？

清晨醒来，消除了一身的疲惫，
有了轻盈的身体，拉开窗帘。
看到阳光照耀着大地，还有"叽叽喳喳"的鸟叫声。
是否感到有一种喜悦、一种阳光明媚？
因为今天出行，你不用带伞、不会堵车，也不会湿鞋。
幸福就在清晨的阳光里。

来到办公室，
在同事的一声问候、一个微笑中开始了紧张的工作。
电话声、会议声、键盘声、打印机声

In the hustle and bustle of the busy world,
We are all in pursuit of happiness.
But it seems to be on the distant horizon, or in the distant future!
O happiness, where is it?

Waking up in the morning, with all the fatigue gone,
Nimbly I pull back the curtains.
Seeing the sun shining and listening to the chirps of birds,
Do you feel a joy, a sunny brightness?
Because you don't have to bring an umbrella with you, and you will not be stuck in a traffic jam or wet your shoes.
Happiness is in the sunshine of early morning.

Arriving at the office,
You start to work in a busy day, with a greeting and a smile from your colleague.
The sound of phone calls, meetings,

此起彼伏。

空隙之际，

泡上一杯清茶或咖啡，一股香气沁入心扉。

望一眼窗外的街道，车水马龙，川流不息。

是否感到有一种舒坦、一种怡然自得？

因为你没有无聊，没有迷茫，也没有忙得不可开交。

幸福就在工作中的一杯清茶或咖啡中。

傍晚回家，远远看到自家窗口有一盏灯光，

还有，牵挂你的人在等你。

孩子已经放学在做作业，

有时还给你开门，欢快地叫你"爸爸"或"妈妈"。

家人已经准备了几个你喜欢吃的家常菜，

那食物的香味诱惑着你的肚子"咕噜咕噜"响。

拿起调羹，喝一口热气腾腾、鲜美的汤，

是否有一种温馨、一种人间烟火味？

因为你没有孤单，没有别离，也没有饥寒交迫。

幸福就在回家的晚餐里。

幸福就是点点滴滴的愉悦，汇聚成一条长河，

keyboards, and printers can be heard here and there.

When taking a break,

You make a cup of tea or coffee, with a refreshing aroma.

You look out of the window at the street with heavy traffic.

Do you feel comfortable and content?

Because you are not bored, not confused, and not terribly busy.

Happiness is in a cup of tea or coffee at work.

Coming home in the evening, you already see the light from a window of your home,

Knowing that people who care about you are waiting for you.

The child is doing the homework after school,

Who will sometimes open the door for you and call you "Dad" or "Mom" cheerfully.

Someone has cooked your favorite dishes,

The smell of which makes your stomach grumble.

Then you pick up a spoon and take a sip of the steaming, delicious soup.

Is there a touching warmth, and a taste of the life?

Because you are not lonely, without parting or poverty.

Happiness is in a dinner at home.

Happiness is a long river formed by myriads of joyful moments,

静静地流淌在普普通通的生活里。

只要有一颗知足的心和一双发现美的眼睛，

幸福，无处不在！

一念天堂，一念地狱，

幸福，就在你的一念间！

Which flows quietly in the ordinary life.

So long as you are not greedy and have an eye for beauty,

Happiness is everywhere!

Heaven and hell are only within a flash of thought.

Happiness is in your mind!

王月平
Ada Wang

2014年加入CNOOD财务部，温柔而坚定，知足而上进。不要为小事遮住视线，我们还有更大的世界！

Ada joined the Finance Department of CNOOD in 2014. She is gentle and strong-willed; She is content but eager to improve. Do not let small things block our sights, because there's a bigger world ahead!

2022 年生活中那些阶段性的思考

2022: Some Reflections at Certain Stages of Life

■ Cassie Chen

我一直以为自己的生活会波澜不惊、按部就班，直到 2022 年的到来。

2022 年 3 月底，家属回老家看娃，我一个人在上海。疫情期间，邻里互助，质朴的善意最大限度地释放，人间烟火气尤令人触动。我不是个性格活络的人，却也在此时深受感召，结识了多年不识的邻居，相互代领物资、送药送菜、加油打气，孤独的灵魂被重重暖意包裹。疫情对世界影响甚巨，人与人的关系同样如此。很多时候，曾经失去的，还会在不经意间，以熟悉的方式重新回到我们身边。

6 月中旬，我正式加入施璐德这个让

Until the year 2022, I always thought my life would be uneventful and orderly.

At the end of March 2022, my husband went back to the hometown to see our kid and I was alone in Shanghai. During the epidemic, neighbors in our community helped each other, demonstrating the simple kindness to the greatest extent. The vibrant urban life seemed to me even more touching. Though not an active person, I was deeply inspired at that time. I got to know my neighbors whom I didn't know in the past years, and we collected supplies for each other, sent medicine and food to each other and cheered on each other. My lonely soul was surrounded by great warmth. The epidemic had a huge impact on the world, as well as on interpersonal relationships. In many cases, what was once lost will come back to us in a familiar way before we notice it.

In the middle of June, I joined

人向往的大家庭，我庆幸能与各位优秀的同事共事，亦深知自己需要学习提升的地方太多太多。初入陌生领域的我慌张无措，深知自己的沟通能力亟待提升；粗心大意造成的失误又常常让我处于懊恼惭愧的境地。幸好得到我们部门无所不能的罗导（Loreen）和有求必应的小吴同学（Liam）的倾力相助，让我能够逐渐稳定下来，工作步入正轨。

半年多的时间里，部门总经理罗导对我悉心指导，批判和鼓励并行。她教会我做事有明确解题思路很重要，一件事除了关注结果，更要理解为何这样操作。如果偏离了正确的方向，只能及时调整并加倍努力，回到正路上来。很多时候在我毫无意识地犯错后，她即便气得够呛，依然还在想着如何帮我弥补错误，事后更是和我一起复盘，找到犯错的原因和改进措施。我感慨自己是幸运的，除了得到罗导的高阶指引，"IT高手"小吴同学的有求必应也是大大缓解了工作中的焦虑。他能搞定一切电子产品的故障报修，同时慷慨地承包各种体力活，生日会采购、新年布置会场……任何时候找他求助，他总能快速顺利地解决。

the attractive big family of CNOOD. I was lucky to work with all the excellent colleagues, knowing that I had a lot to learn. I was often at a loss when I first entered this unfamiliar field, and I needed to improve my communication skills. I was upset and abashed because of the mistakes I made due to carelessness. Luckily, bit by bit, I settled into the new job and got on track with the selfless help from Loreen who is omnipotent, and Liam, who is ready to help whenever I ask him for a favor.

For more than half a year, Loreen, the general manager of our department, guided me meticulously, with both criticism and encouragement. She taught me that it is important to have a clear idea of how to solve a problem, and that we should pay more attention to why we dealt with a matter in a certain way rather than focusing on the results. If we deviate from the right direction, we have no choice but to make timely adjustments and redouble our efforts to come back to the right track. Sometimes, though she was extremely angry when I made a mistake inadvertently, she would still think about the way of helping me make up for the mistake and would later review the case with me to find the reasons for my mistake and improvement measures. I thought I was lucky, besides the high-level guidance from Loreen, the responsiveness of Liam the "IT expert" greatly relieved my anxiety in the work. He could fix all the electronic products and generously took up all kinds of manual work, such as

虽然人生在世，总有不如意，但我在动荡不安的2022年收获良多。时常提醒自己，永远要抱有感恩之心，在鲜活的2023年，与好运同行。

birthday party procurement, arrangement of the New Year party venue ... Every time I ask him for help, he will always get it done quickly.

Life is not a bed of roses. Nevertheless, I have gained a lot in the uneasy year of 2022. I often remind myself to be always grateful. May I walk with good fortune in the lively year of 2023.

陈劲草 Cassie Chen	疾风知劲草，板荡识诚臣。 As the force of the wind tests the strength of grass, so a man proves his loyalty in times of turbulence.

2023 春节有感

The Spring Festival of 2023

■ Liam Wu

记忆中的年味，是挂在老房子墙上的那本黄历每天都在变薄，它的封面是喜庆的中国红，白底黑字的纸张上写满了农历、阳历、节气和各种宜忌事项等。每年的最后一个月都是数着日子等着新年的到来。随着时间的推移，心情也愈来愈迫切与激动。

记忆中的年味，是大年三十在外婆家度过一整天。早上开始买春联、红灯笼、鞭炮、爆竹，年夜饭的食材一般提前好几天就会准备好，而外婆也是一大早就在烧年夜饭。快到中午的时候，长辈就开始准备贴春联和门神了，中堂的新年画也会挂上。做完这些后外公外婆就会坐在桌子的上席，等着晚辈们磕头拜年。接下来就是关上大门吃年夜饭了，当然关门之前还需要放一串鞭炮，吃完饭才能再打开门，寓意着"闭门生财、开门大吉"。

The Spring Festival, in my memory, was the time when the lunar almanac hanging on the wall of the old house got thinner every day. The almanac, with its festive Chinese-red cover, contained the lunar and solar calendars, solar terms, and various dos and don'ts according to traditional beliefs. In the last month of each year, people counted the days when waiting for the lunar New Year. As time went by, people became more and more eager and excited.

The Spring Festival, in my memory, was the time when I spent a whole day at Grandma's home on lunar New Year's Eve. In the morning, we went out to buy Spring Festival couplets, red lanterns, and firecrackers. The ingredients for the New Year's Eve dinner were usually prepared several days in advance, and Grandma began to cook the dinner early in the morning. When it was almost noon, the elder members of the family would start

记忆中的年味，是除夕夜守旧，父母忙着卤煮食物，而我就吃着零食看着春晚。当除夕夜的钟声敲响之后，震耳欲聋的烟花便开始争奇斗艳，家家户户都点燃了鞭炮，空气里四处都弥漫着硫磺的气味。窗外的烟花时而像金菊绽放、牡丹怒开；时而像彩蝶翩跹、巨龙腾飞；时而像火树银花、绚丽漫舞；时而像漫天流星，一闪而逝，简直让人眼花缭乱、目不暇接。仿佛整个世界都淹没在烟花的海洋里，寄托着人们对未来的美好愿望。正是"万炮齐鸣震九天，金龙彩凤舞翩然"。

to hang up the Spring Festival couplets and the pictures of door-gods, as well as the New Year picture in the central room. After that, my grandparents would sit in the seats of honor at the table and wait for the younger generation to kowtow with New Year greetings. Then we closed the door to have the New Year's Eve dinner, before which we let off a string of firecrackers, and we could not open the door again until we finished the dinner, meaning "close the door to produce wealth, and open the door for great luck."

The Spring Festival, in my memory, was the time when we stayed up all night on the lunar New Year's Eve. My parents would be busy stewing food in special sauce, while I was eating snacks and watching the Spring Festival Gala. When the New Year bell rang, the fireworks with their deafening sound began to contend for beauty and fascination. As every household lit firecrackers, the air was filled with the smell of sulfur. The fireworks outside the window were sometimes like golden chrysanthemums and peonies in full bloom, sometimes like dancing butterflies and soaring dragons; sometimes like fiery trees and silver flowers swaying brilliantly, sometimes like shooting stars streaking across the sky. They formed so many dazzling scenes that we simply could not watch them all. The whole world seemed to be submerged in a sea of fireworks, expressing people's good wishes for the future.

记忆中的年味，是能带来欢声笑语的小品，是优美的舞蹈，是动听的歌声，是神奇的魔术，也是老一辈艺术家们的精彩表演。《钟点工》《卖拐》《卖车》《功夫》《飞天》《梦幻家园》等节目仿佛还历历在目。

每当夜深人静无法入眠的时候，那些儿时的欢乐时刻，那些尘封已久的记忆便如潮水般向我涌来，让我不由自主地想到"花有重开日，人无再少年"。

Indeed:

Ten thousand firecrackers splutter in unison, as if shaking the sky,

And with grace the golden dragon and the gorgeous phoenix dance.

The Spring Festival, in my memory, was the time when we enjoyed the TV skits that brought cheers and laughter, the graceful dances, the lovely voice of singing, the mysterious magic, and the wonderful performances of veteran artists, among which "An Hourly Worker," "Selling the Crutches," "Selling a Bicycle," "Kung Fu," "Flying Apsaras," "The Dream Home," etc., seem to be still fresh in my mind.

Whenever I cannot fall asleep in the depth of night, sealed memories of those childhood joy would flood over me, and I can't help but think of the lines, "A flower may blossom again, but youth never returns."

吴祖亮
Liam Wu

单身，编程发烧友。
Single, Programming enthusiast.

2022 年有感
My Reflections on 2022

■ Danni Xu

2022年部门工作逐渐步入正轨，作为职能部门，2023年我们要继续思考如何更好地为业务团队服务，为公司助力。

一、从部门自身入手，提升专业度

首先，我们要知道业务团队需要什么样的支持而我们能提供什么样的帮助，我们的亮点是什么。

2022年在公司的支持和部门的努力下，我们争取到交通银行香港分行1亿美金的授信额度，在投融资板块实现了新的突破。但我们仍需关注，目前的额度和业务是否匹配，每年能否完成循环使用，未来需要争取什么类型的额度或更加优惠的条件。

The work of our department gradually went onto the right track in 2022. In 2023, we, as a functional department, will keep thinking about how we could better serve business teams and help boost the growth of the company.

I. Enhance Professionalism, Starting from Our Department

First, we must know what kind of support the business teams need as well as what kind of help we can offer, and what we are good at doing.

In 2022, we secured a credit line of 100 million US dollars from the Bank of Communications Hong Kong Branch with the support of the company and the efforts of our department, achieving a new breakthrough in investment and financing. Nevertheless, attention must still be paid to whether the current line of credit matches our business, whether

合规虽然没有实现全面"中国化",对于我们这样的企业而言,却是不可或缺的一部分。在越来越多的投标项目或是供应商注册中,客户开始关注我们是否拥有完善的合规体系、制度。目前我司合规体系已运营近1年,并在不断实践中优化完善。合规之路道阻且长,需要我们不断探索,将合规落实到日常经营管理的每一步。

其次,在履行岗位职责方面,我们目前能给自己打多少分?还有多少进步的空间?

2022年,我们结合公司的发展现状完善了部门的岗位职能。目前投融资、合规、风控板块已初具雏形,但是其中的薄弱项也颇为明显。比如保险方面,在业务同事咨询的时候,我们更多地依赖于保险公司专业老师的解答。由于国内外保险体系的不同和条款的差异,我们时常无法满足客户的相关要求。2023年,我们计划针对保险方面开展针对性的培训,拓宽保险渠道,并进一步加强与业务同事的沟通,从沟通中发掘机会、发现问题。

we can make the best use of the revolving credit limit, and what type of credit line or more favourable terms we need to seek in the future.

Though not yet fully localized in China, compliance is an indispensable part of the business for companies like ours. In more and more bidding projects or supplier registrations, concerns are raised about whether we have a sound compliance system in place. Now our compliance system has been in operation for almost one year and is being constantly optimized and improved. The way is long and difficult, but we shall keep exploring and carrying out compliance requirements in every detail of daily management.

Second, how would we rate ourselves on job responsibilities at present? How much room is there for improvement?

In 2022, we improved the functions of our department, taking into account the current development of the company. Now, functions including investment and financing, compliance and risk control have taken shape, but with obvious weaknesses. As regards insurance affairs, for instance, we rely heavily on professionals from insurance companies to answer the questions of our colleagues from business teams. Due to the differences in domestic and international insurance systems and terms, it often happens that we cannot meet our customers' relevant demands. We plan to carry out targeted training on insurance in 2023, develop more channels

二、从本部门与其他部门的工作交接入手，实现强强联合

首先，本部门工作的开展有赖于其他部门的配合，比如合规工作。合规是一项较新的工作，我们需要让它融入现有的工作中。在涉及招待、培训等事项时，需要全体员工的配合。针对尽调、投标、员工入职等事项时，需要不同部门分工协作，让合规的要求和部门原有的操作流程融洽地结合起来。在这个过程中，我们遇到了很多挑战，复杂的要求、冗长的流程让原本习惯性的任务增加了新的工作量。我们乐于接受大家提出的意见或建议，并在合规框架下优化流程。但完善是长期的过程，我们仍需各部门的积极支持和大力配合。

其次，为了更好地发挥部门之间的联动性，我们要更加积极地参与项目的全流程。比如在和设计技术/项目管理部合作

of insurance, and further enhance communication with colleagues from business teams, whereby we may identify opportunities as well as problems.

II. Achieve Synergy, Starting from the Work Interface Between Our Department and Other Departments

First, we depend upon the cooperation of other departments in conducting the work of our department, such as that of compliance. As a relatively new job, compliance needs to be integrated into the existing work. When it comes to matters such as hospitality and training, we need the cooperation of all the staff. For matters such as due diligence, bidding and new employees' on-boarding process, we need different departments to work together so that compliance requirements would fit in well with the existing operational processes. We encountered many challenges, while complicated requirements and lengthy processes led to extra workload in addition to routine tasks. We are willing to accept comments or suggestions and will optimize the process within the compliance framework. However, it is a long-term process to achieve the improvement, during which we still need the active support and cooperation of all departments.

Second, we need to take a more active part in the whole process of any project to give full play to the inter-departmental

投标项目时，除了协助尽调、投标合规等工作外，我们也会更多地参与项目的各个环节，及时提示风险，以防范未来可能出现的问题，保障公司稳健发展。

三、从团队培养入手，提升团队协作能力

我们在做 2022 年总结时，复盘了一整年的工作得失，团队内部也完成了自评和互评。借此，我们明确了个人需要改进的地方，确立了工作重点以及需要部门支持、团队配合的方面。

我们希望部门每个人都能拥有自己的职业规划，并在修正完善中成长为独当一面的部门业务骨干。2022 年，我们编纂了部门内部操作手册，用以培养新人。如果新人没有方向，就先以部门的方向为方向，熟识部门事务，在有余力的条件下横向拓展部门职能，或纵向增强部门的专业度。我们相信个人方向与部门方向并不矛盾，两者相辅相成，个人的方向有时亦能成为部门的方向。

linkage. For example, when working with the Engineering & Project Management Department on bidding projects, in addition to assisting with due diligence and bidding compliance, we will be involved to a greater extent in all aspects of the project and warn against risks promptly to prevent possible problems and safeguard the steady development of the company.

III. Enhance Teamwork Ability, Starting from Team Training

When doing the annual summary of 2022, we reviewed the gains and losses in our work throughout the year and completed self-assessment and mutual assessment within the team as well. In this way, we identified areas for personal improvement, priorities in our work, and aspects in which we need departmental support and teamwork.

We hope that all members in our department will have their own career planning and, through revision and refinement, become the backbone of the department who are able to shoulder responsibilities alone. In 2022, we compiled an internal operating manual for the training of newcomers. If a newcomer does not have a direction, he or she should first take the direction of the department, become familiar with the business of the department and, if possible, expand departmental functions horizontally or enhance the department's professionalism vertically. We believe that personal direction and departmental direction are not contradictory, but complementary to each other, while personal direction can sometimes become the direction of the department.

2016 年 4 月正式加入施璐德，成为施璐德大家庭的一名成员。作为一只小金牛，爱财且取之有道。渴望拥有吃喝玩乐的生活和充实的精神世界，并为此不懈努力。

徐丹妮
Danni Xu

Danni joined CNOOD in April 2016 and became a member of the investment and financing department. She longs to have an enjoyable material life and an affluent spiritual life and is making unremitting efforts to achieve these.

笃行逐梦　不负韶华

Be Honest in Your Pursuit of Dreams, and Waste Not the Days of Youth

■ Heather Zhang

有备无患

2022年12月初，大家都开始囤药，我和先生都比较佛系，家里还有一些药，所以就没有囤。由于各路消息在网络传播迅速，在老家的爸妈跟风买了好多感冒药，用我爸爸的话说："花钱买个安心，也可以分给亲戚朋友，用不到最好！"

Better Safe Than Sorry

At the beginning of December 2022, everyone started to stock up on medicines. With the mentality of "que será, será" and some medicine at home, my husband and I didn't stock up. As information spread really fast on the Internet, my parents who lived in the hometown followed suit and bought quite a lot of cold medicine. As Dad said, "We spent money for the peace of mind, and we can give them out to our relatives and friends. It's best if we don't have to take them!"

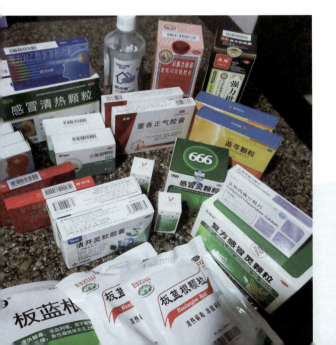

疫情3年，特别是2022年，我们真是经历了太多，最大的感受就是有备无患很重要，生活物资是，钱财积蓄也是，健康的身体更是。

追求专业

池总在公司的2022年度总结大会上，提出要重视"赛道的选择与角色的提升"。公司汇集了各种专业的人才，有做传统业务的，有做矿业的，有做半导体行业的，有做光伏的。这个世界是瞬息万变的，个人唯有顺应外界的变化，主动变化，选择真正适合的赛道，方能确保自身始终行进在正确的轨道之中。

我的理解是，不管处在哪条赛道，追求专业是一个长期永恒的目标。时时刻刻都要做到专业，我接触的人才会信任我、愿意把事情交给我。追求专业的过程也是一次次角色提升的过程。可以把个人的专业能力理解成个人IP，打造个人IP的过程就是持续倒逼自己不断学习升级，才能不被这个社会淘汰。

我反思自己在面对困难时，是否消耗太多的时间与情绪在前期的铺垫上，最后

We have undergone too much during the past three years affected by epidemic, especially in 2022. Our strongest feeling is that it's important to be always prepared. This is true with life supplies, money, and above all, our health.

The Pursuit of Professionalism

At the annual meeting of 2022, Dennis emphasized the importance of "the selection of fields and the upgrading of our roles". CNOOD has pooled a galaxy of professional talents, who are working in traditional businesses as well as mining, semiconductor or photovoltaic industries. In a rapidly changing world, we can be sure that we are always on the right track only by adapting to external changes, taking the initiative to make changes and choosing the truly suitable field.

The pursuit of professionalism, as I understand it, is a long-term and perennial goal no matter which field we are in. I must be professional all the time so that people would trust me, willing to leave matters to me. Time and again we experience upgrading of roles in pursuing professionalism. The professional capabilities of a person can be viewed as the personal IP, and the creation of such IP means forcing ourselves to continuously learn and improve in order to stand the test of the society.

Reflecting on my work, I wonder whether I have wasted too much time

还得直面问题，花大力气去解决它。现在遇到问题，我会在心里提醒自己，不要被情绪左右，静下来分析问题，用专业的态度去思考。只有行动了才知道成不成。不仅要把活干了，还要干得专业。

2023年注定是奋斗的一年，"路漫漫其修远兮"，愿我们笃行逐梦、不负韶华，迎接属于自己的精彩未来。

and emotion in preparation when facing difficulties. In the end, I still have to put in great effort to solve the problems that cannot be avoided. Now I will remind myself, when I meet with a problem, to calm down and analyze the problem with professionalism, rather than be swayed by emotions. We can know the result only when we do it. Not only do we have to do the job, but we should also do it in a professional way.

The year 2023 is destined to be a year of endeavor, with a long, long way ahead. May we be honest in pursuit of our dreams and never waste the good days of youth, greeting the wonderful future that belongs to us.

张霄燕
Heather Zhang

中共党员，上海对外经贸大学硕士，于2014年加入施璐德。

Heather is a Party member, who graduated from Shanghai University of International Business and Economics with a master's degree and joined CNOOD in 2014.

回首 2022 年
Looking Back on 2022

Jodie Zhou

走过 2022 年，再回首，思考多，感慨多，收获也多。

回首 2022 年，这是不平凡的一年。这一年，有成长，有喜悦，也有过迷茫，但最终得以释怀，淡然从容地回首、充满希望的期待。

回首 2022 年，与部门一起优化、运行合规体系，落实各项合规制度，对合规风险进行持续监测和评估，提供合规整改意见，保证公司健康稳健地发展。这里面有我们摸索的过程，也记载着我们逐步成长为一支专业合规团队的足迹，教会了我发挥团队精神的重要性，团结协作、发挥所长。在工作中，团队精神就是大局意识、协作精神和服务精神的集中体现。个人力量是有限的，集体的力量是无穷的。一个团队里，每个人都有擅长的领域，在尊重个人所长的基础上，明确协作方式，统一个体发展和团队整体发展，朝着一个共同的目标努力，这样才能保证集体的高效率运转，才能充分发挥团队的潜能。

When I look back on the year 2022, I cannot help but think a lot while being deeply moved with many fruitful results.

Looking back on 2022, I find it to be an extraordinary year. It was a year of growth, joy and confusion, but in the end we are able to let go of it and look back with calmness and hopeful expectation.

Looking back on 2022, I recall how I worked with my department to optimize and run the compliance system, implement compliance regulations, conduct continuous monitoring and evaluation of compliance risks and provide rectification advice to ensure the healthy and steady growth of the company. This included the process of trial and error and our footprints in the way of becoming a professional compliance team. I was taught the importance of team spirit, i.e. working with others and giving full play to one's strength. At work, team spirit is the embodiment of big-picture

回首 2022 年，我学会工作应不拘于常规化，而应培养开拓和主动精神。在个人的成长阶段，必须要有开拓的勇气，具备创新的能力，善于接受新鲜事物，善于提出新设想、新方案，对每年的工作都要有新目标、新追求。同时，也要将创新与实践相结合，将开拓方向与部门职能相统一，不天马行空，更脚踏实地。

回首 2022 年，或悲伤，或欣喜，或快乐。展望 2023 年，愿我们仍是追梦人，未来之路道阻且长，愿你我戮力同心，携手同行，一起迎接更加精彩纷呈的 2023 年！

thinking, the spirit of collaboration and the spirit of service. The strength of any individual is limited, while the power of a team is infinite. In a team, everyone has an area of expertise. While respecting individual strengths, we clarify the way of collaboration, integrate the development of each member and that of the team as a whole, and work together towards a common goal to ensure the efficient operation of the organization and make best of the potential of the team.

Looking back on 2022, I have been taught that we should not be limited to routines in our work and the pioneering spirit and initiative should be developed. In the stages of personal growth, we must have the courage to break new ground with the ability to innovate, ready to embrace new things and good at bringing forward new ideas and new programs, with new goals for each year in our work. Meanwhile, it is necessary to integrate innovation with practice, synergizing the direction in exploring new frontiers with the functions of our department. We should be down-to-earth instead of indulging in wild fantasies.

Looking back on 2022, we are filled with sadness, joy or happiness. May we still be dream catchers in 2023. Though the journey ahead is difficult and long, may we work together, hand in hand, to meet a more exciting and colorful year in 2023!

中南财经政法大学金融硕士,一个地道的无辣不欢的湖北人,一个捕获到美食便能开心一天的金牛座。时刻相信生活充满无限可能,并一直用乐观、开朗的态度面对工作和生活!

周 颖
Jodie Zhou

Master of Finance from Zhongnan University of Economics and Law, Jodie is a Hubei native who extremely loves spicy food, a Taurus who can have a good day when she enjoys delicious food. She always believes that life is full of possibilities and always maintains an optimistic and cheerful attitude towards work and life!

四十不惑

At the Age of Forty

■ James Zhu

2023年新的一年，新的时光，新的气象，每个人都在义无反顾地向前走着，不管前方是坦途还是曲折。但我们希望每一年都会有新的改变，新的收获，新的人和事出现。

2023年新的一年，是开心、喜庆、不平常的一年。新春的烟火驱散了疫情的阴霾，向往已久的繁华与热闹开始恢复，一片生机勃勃的景象又呈现在眼前，我想这是所有人期盼已久的时刻。2023年新年，不但要总结过往，还要筹划未来，每个人都计划着在新的一年努力奋斗，奋斗出新的成绩、新的奇迹。

一转眼，自己不再年少，不惑之年悄然来到，生活的琐碎，吐出来矫情，吞下去呛嗓子；百般滋味涌上心头。我的青春

2023 shall see new days and new scenes. Everyone is marching forward without the least hesitation, whether the journey ahead is straight or tortuous. But we still hope that we will see new changes and have new harvests every year, with new people and new things.

2023 will be a joyful, festive and extraordinary year. With the firecrackers of Spring Festival dispelling the shadows of the COVID-19 epidemic, the long-awaited hustle and bustle begins to come back with a scene of vigor unfolding before us. It is, I think, a moment that all of us have been looking forward to. At the beginning of 2023, we not only take stock of the past, but also plan for the future. Everyone is planning for the endeavors in the coming year; through these endeavors, we are going to have new achievements and make new miracles.

I'm no longer young before I know it. I'm reaching the age of forty. I would be fussy if I vent my frustration about the

彻底结束了，我们低估了时间的善变，让原本浓烈的东西轻易地翻了篇。40岁是自渡的年龄，我开始变得不悲不喜，懂得善良中带点锋芒，懂得热爱家庭和生活。

时间终教会我们，万事藏于心，而不表于情。有风听风，下雨看雨，生活并没有深意，幸福和遗憾都藏在日常里。

2023年加油！为自己，为家人，为朋友，为所有努力前行的人。

trivialities of life, but would choke if I just swallow it. My heart is filled with a myriad of mixed feelings. My youth has ended for ever. We have underestimated the fickleness of time, getting over something that used to be strong. Now at forty, an age of self-salvation, I started to become neither sad nor happy. I have learned to be assertive while being kind, and to love my family and life.

Eventually, time will teach us to keep all things to ourselves instead of showing them on the face. Listen to the wind when there is wind, and enjoy the rain when it rains. Life does not run deep, with all happiness and regret embedded in daily routines.

Go for it in 2023! For myself, for my family, for my friends, and for all those who are trying their best to march forward.

朱 建 / James Zhu

2016年加入施璐德。

James joined CNOOD in 2016.

图书在版编目(CIP)数据

施璐德年鉴.2022:汉、英/施璐德亚洲有限公司编;岑品杰译.—上海:复旦大学出版社,
2023.11
ISBN 978-7-309-16885-3

Ⅰ.①施… Ⅱ.①施… ②岑… Ⅲ.①建筑企业-上海-2022-年鉴-汉、英 Ⅳ.①F426.9-54

中国国家版本馆 CIP 数据核字(2023)第 104487 号

施璐德年鉴 2022

SHILUDE NIANJIAN 2022
施璐德亚洲有限公司　编
译者/岑品杰
责任编辑/谢同君　李　荃

复旦大学出版社有限公司出版发行
上海市国权路 579 号　邮编:200433
网址:fupnet@fudanpress.com　http://www.fudanpress.com
门市零售:86-21-65102580　团体订购:86-21-65104505
出版部电话:86-21-65642845
上海丽佳制版印刷有限公司

开本 787 毫米×1092 毫米　1/16　印张 12.5　字数 281 千字
2023 年 11 月第 1 版
2023 年 11 月第 1 版第 1 次印刷

ISBN 978-7-309-16885-3/F・2982
定价:88.00 元

如有印装质量问题,请向复旦大学出版社有限公司出版部调换。
版权所有　侵权必究